TEN MONTHS IN BRAZIL.

ENTRANCE TO RIO DE JANEIRO.—Page 39.

TEN MONTHS IN BRAZIL:

WITH

NOTES ON THE PARAGUAYAN WAR.

BY

JOHN CODMAN.

SECOND EDITION.

NEW YORK:
JAMES MILLER, PUBLISHER,
647 BROADWAY.

1872.

TO

MY WIFE AND DAUGHTER,

WHO HAVE SO OFTEN BEEN MY COMPANIONS ON THE OCEAN AND IN FOREIGN LANDS,

This Souvenir of our Visit to Brazil

IS AFFECTIONATELY INSCRIBED.

PREFACE TO THE SECOND AMERICAN EDITION.

THERE have been some changes since the first edition of this work was published.

St. Thomas has been devastated by earthquakes and hurricanes; the Paraguayan war has come to an end; slavery is being abolished in Brazil. Otherwise, the value of the book, whatever that may be, remains the same.

CONTENTS.

CHAPTER I.

CHAPTER II.

CHAPTER III.

CHAPTER IV.

CHAPTER V.

CHAPTER VI.

CHAPTER VII.

CHAPTER VIII.

CHAPTER IX.

CHAPTER X.

CHAPTER XI.

CHAPTER XII.

CHAPTER XIII.

CHAPTER XIV.

CHAPTER XV.

CHAPTER XVI.

CHAPTER XVII.

CHAPTER XVIII.

CHAPTER XIX.

CHAPTER XX.

TEN MONTHS IN BRAZIL.

CHAPTER I.

Commencement of the Voyage. — Sailors' Superstitions. — Tossing in the Gulf Stream. — Effects of Sea-sickness. — Arrival at St. Thomas. — Condition of the Negroes. — Results of Emancipation. — Female Coal-Carriers. — A Black Squall. — The Captain in Peril. — Rescue by an African Goddess.

ON Friday, the 2d of December, 1864, the steamer "Cotopaxi" lifted her anchor and proceeded to sea, from New York. All the world knows that Friday is an "unlucky day." I should be ashamed to admit a belief in the superstition, but I will confess that if I had the choice of a sailing day, it would not be Friday. A sufficient reason is, its depressing influence upon a crew when any accident occurs. If it be a serious one, calling upon all their energies to save the ship, one last effort, which might have been successful, may not be made, because of the remembrance that "she sailed on Friday." The influence of the day was not perceptible upon the comfort and pleasure of the voyage to St. Thomas. The passengers were generally tropic birds, who had flown to the north for a summer visit, and were driven home by the first blasts of winter. There were some pretty Spanish girls among them, who were returning to Porto Rico. With them the young gentlemen managed to while away the passage of a week so agreeably, that they wished it might have been a month or a year.

On the second day after leaving New York, we entered the Gulf Stream. As the ship was light, and her coal stowed below, she was excessively uneasy; for the wind had freshened into an easterly gale, and a boiling cross-sea was the consequence. Passengers and dishes, negro waiters and baggage, were knocked about indiscriminately. Lamps were upset, and the oil mingled with the water as prayers mingled with curses. "O Lord," prayed old Mrs. M., "have mercy upon us! Here we are, in the Gulf Stream, at the mercy of the winds and waves, and the captain has gone to sleep! O Lord, have mercy on us!" Libellous old woman, to tell the good Lord such a story about me! Was I not, at the moment you gave utterance to this, — was I not then in the state-room next to yours, holding the head of the charming Matilda, and telling the lovely Rosita that there was no danger, notwithstanding all your noise?

There is no better master of ceremonies on shipboard than sea-sickness. It is a leveller of all distinctions. An immediate intimacy springs up among a crowd of passengers, which is promoted by the absence of all those artificial barriers which society on shore has erected to keep social intercourse within bounds. Sea-sickness demolishes all these at a blow. Hoops, head-dresses, and sometimes false teeth, disappear for the time being, and ladies change from dolls to women. Age and youth are much alike then in appearance and in attractions. Thus it was that my attention to the lovely Spanish girls was purely Platonic and philanthropic. I would have done as much for Mrs. M., if she had not insulted me in her devotions.

Having been thus introduced to each other in the Gulf Stream, the acquaintance of the passengers ripened into friendship, with a dash or so of love, under the genial influences of the balmy trade-winds, and of that lovers' lantern, which, from time immemorial, has hung in the heavens for their theme of poetry. A few musical instruments and many musical voices contributed to the pleasure of all, as we danced merrily along over the silver-crested waves.

The miseries of the Gulf Stream were forgotten, and those who there looked back upon the comforts of home, envious of the friends they had left behind, were now happy in their own enjoyment, congratulating themselves upon escaping the winter which others were obliged to endure. Thus pleasantly passed the last five days of our passage. On the morning of the 9th of December, the high lands of St. Thomas and Porto Rico hove in sight, and after threading the somewhat intricate channel to the eastward of the latter island, we entered the harbor of "Charlotte Amelie," on the south side of St. Thomas, and anchored soon after noon.

St. Thomas is a Danish possession, and with Santa Cruz and a few rocky islets, most of which are uninhabited, constitutes the great West Indian territory of the large and important kingdom of Denmark. Santa Cruz may still be called a Danish island, where the Danish language is spoken. From its fertile soil a considerable revenue is derived for the Danish crown. Those of our passengers who were bound thither to spend the winter according to their custom, described it as almost a paradise, with a luxuriant vegetation and a salubrious climate, so that we could not but regret that it was not in our power to pay it at least a flying visit. The communication between the islands is, however, irregular and uncertain, for lack of steamers. It is confined to small schooners, which sometimes make the passage across in a few hours, and sometimes in a few days. From all that we could learn, the island is a very desirable residence in the winter for invalids, and the line of steamers to Rio de Janeiro, touching at St. Thomas, being established, Santa Cruz will doubtless become a fashionable resort.

The Island of St. Thomas, though small in extent, — about fifteen miles long and five miles wide, — contains a great deal of arable and fertile soil, little of which is now cultivated. The inhabitants depend upon the neighboring Island of Porto Rico for nearly all their cattle, poultry, fruit, and vegetables. Before slavery was abolished, not only did St. Thomas supply all these for their own consumption, when the population far exceeded the present, but it produced thousands of hogsheads of sugar, molasses, and rum for exportation. Riding over the island, we constantly passed the ruins of plantation-houses and sheds, of sugar-mills and distilleries. The negroes are said to have been well treated, and not overworked, and were, therefore, in accordance with what was considered their place upon the scale of creation, in the possession of such happiness as their limited faculties would permit them to enjoy. They have now nearly disappeared from the back country. A few miserable wretches remain, scattered here and there, who live upon wild fruits and roots, and by thieving. When these resources fail, they descend to the town and obtain employment, which they can always do with ease. They will work long enough, and no longer than is necessary to insure them against starvation for a month or so ahead, and then they return to their huts. Labor is at all times remunerative in the town, and it is mainly on this account that the plantations are universally abandoned, as the planters have found it useless to compete with the slave labor of Porto Rico, or the free labor of Santa Cruz, where no such facilities for obtaining high wages are enjoyed by the blacks.

St. Thomas, from its situation in the group of Windward Islands (being in the track of trade between Europe and the other West India Islands, Mexico, Central America, and the Spanish Main), cannot be otherwise than of great commercial importance. Its harbor is the best in all the Windward Islands, and is secure from the danger of the terrible hurricanes which prevail chiefly in the summer and autumn. For these reasons, whenever a ship is heard of in distress anywhere upon the broad Atlantic, the next news from her may be expected from St. Thomas. When the sails are blown to shreds, the pump-bolts worn with friction, and the crew "used up," the captain is at length discouraged and down-hearted with useless beating and banging to the westward. Then, in a tone of despair, he gives the order, "Up helm and square away for St. Thomas." Down glides the tired ship through the fairy regions of the gentle trades, where the zephyrs of eternal summer blow. The captain, passengers, and crew creep out into sunshine, and as the ship rolls along under her tattered rags, they spread themselves lazily upon the decks, and dream *dolce far niente*-ly of pineapples, oranges, bananas, and all the numberless luxuries of the tropics. The underwriters at home, when they hear of it, sleep with nightmares on their breasts, and with visions of poverty on their brains.

The discharging and reloading of these vessels in distress furnish employment for hundreds of negroes. Many of the more intelligent are engaged upon the repairs. All are well paid, as the enormous profits gained by the contractors' agents and mechanics enable them to share a part of their gains with their laborers. For the most common work the pay is one dollar and a quarter per day in silver.

The work upon coal at St. Thomas is done exclusively by women; and when the number of steamers calling at this port, and of ships which bring their supplies, is considered, the labor which the women perform is almost incredible. When we were ready for our coal, and the stages rigged, these women threw into the hold on the first day over three hundred tons. Each of them brought upon her head a basket of the average weight of eighty pounds. They came in single file, in one continual stream, like an army of black ants. As they dumped the contents of their baskets, they passed around the hatchways, and returned to the dock by the other plank of the stage, avoiding those who were coming on board. Most of them were horrid hags. The absence of good-looking women among them is readily accounted for by the loose morality of the people, which enables such to support their existence in better accordance with their own tastes. In our country we have heard much of the licentiousness emanating from slavery. It remains to be seen if the morals of our blacks will be improved by its abolition. If there was greater depravity in St. Thomas in the days of bondage than now, a degree of comparison beyond the superlative must be used to express it. With the exception of these women, who were too ugly for such employment as others found most congenial, and were accordingly used as beasts of burden, it is not far from the truth to say that every black woman on the island is a prostitute.

There are exceptions to all rules; and when I speak of the seventy-five women employed on the "Cotopaxi," I do not include as among the uglies the tawny, shining, bright-eyed, straight-limbed combination of the African Venus and the Grecian Minerva, Joanna. What though she carried a basket of coal upon her head — it was a crown of black diamonds there! though her classical only garment was but a strip of gunny cloth encircling her loins — it left unadorned nature free to display the charms of her rounded contour. Joanna, my African princess, decked with the shining dust from the gems of Newcastle and of Cardiff! was I in love with thee? No; but I am grateful; and gratitude to woman is best shown by praising her personal charms.

Some of the women brought more dirt than coal in their baskets. For a time I remonstrated with the contractor, who still persisted in sending on board this refuse of the coal-yard. Without reflecting upon the excitable nature of women in general, black women in particular, and of seventy-five black women combined, I went upon the loading stage and attempted to arrest the further entrance of the Amazons. I stood merely upon the defensive. But they were not to be stopped in this way. One lady pushed a lady against me; another pushed her; till, losing the equipoise of the baskets, several of them went over into the water together. With the splash of the coal there went up simultaneously a tremendous black squall — seventy-five women became seventy-five Hecates; and these were seemingly multiplied into seven hundred and fifty hell-cats! The white overseer came running on board, and besought me to go below, for the attacking column was pressing on to the decks, each virago with a lump of coal in her hand; so that my days seemed to be numbered. In such a crisis, reason quickly balances different courses of action. Run or stay? Run! If there were seventy-five men in front of one, there were illustrious precedents in the Union and rebel ranks for "retreating in good order." Run! Retreat before one woman in a matrimonial battle? Yes, occasionally — generally — I may say, always. But in this case, where I had engaged myself for life to no such obedience — no! never! So I stood my ground, — my deck, — fronting the glaring eyes of the women, and the uplifted missiles of coal. The storm was about to burst, when Joanna threw herself before me, and stretching forth her arms, as when the form of Webster or of Clay arose before the chattering magpies of the Senate, she produced silence ere she spoke a syllable. Then she began with an eloquence of words and of gesticulation which, as it ran on in a stream like that of a leaping cascade, caused one lump of coal after another to drop. Rage changed to hysterics; hysterics, like the after-squalls of a gale, subsided with gentle showers to a calm, and all was peace. The women went again to their work. The contractor sent us no more dirt, and a substantial expression of gratitude to my deliveress was not wanting on my part.

We were told that, a few weeks before, on account of some insult, real or fancied, offered to one of the women by an officer of a Spanish gunboat, which was coaling at this wharf, four or five hundred of these female savages, who were at work on different vessels, dropped their baskets, rushed on board the man-of-war, and obliged the whole crew to take to their boats, some of them being severely wounded.

CHAPTER II.

Climate of St. Thomas. — Yellow Fever. — Modes of Travelling. — A Ride to the Hills. — A Little Denmark. — Visit to Santa Anna. — His Appearance and Conversation. — His Prophecies.

ALTHOUGH it was now the month of December, the weather was intensely hot. We were left to imagine what it might be in summer. The town is situated at the head of a small bay, the entrance to which is from the south, so that the sun, striking upon the glassy water in front, and reflecting from the high hills in the rear, which entirely shut off north and east winds, makes the little settlement the focus of his direct and inverted rays. Yellow fever is an annual visitant, and is merciless in its attacks upon strangers. Even now it had not entirely disappeared, for it prevailed among the shipping, some of the vessels having lost their entire crews.

There are about fifteen thousand inhabitants upon the island, most of whom are concentrated in the town. A long, narrow street runs by the water side, with warehouses and wharves on one hand,

and retail shops upon the other. All the business is transacted here. Three little hills are in the background, towards which run steep alleys, some of them cut into steps, and all of them impassable by carriages. Of these, there are not more than a half dozen on the island. What little travelling is done, is upon horses or mules. Behind these three hills, one of which is surmounted by the governor's palace, and the others clustered upon by the wealthier inhabitants, rise the high peaks, upon which graze the only cattle that are kept on the island, and where a few gentlemen, not too lazy to climb, have perched themselves and their families, with a due regard to health.

Mr. Sonderburg, who lived upon the highest point of St. Thomas, asked us to breakfast with him one morning. The traveller goes to Europe and finds his enjoyment in the Louvre, and in the palaces and galleries of Florence and of Rome. A thousand times more do I prefer such a morning's ride after a week's voyage. The freshness of the open air, instead of the confined atmosphere of a palace; the song of the birds, instead of the rustling of catalogues and of dresses; the clatter of hoofs, instead of the noiseless carpet tread; and, above all, the great panorama of nature—the sun rising from his water-bed, shaking off the drops in slanting showers, then breaking out and multiplying himself a million times in rain and dew-drops, throwing ever-varying shadows and streams of light from mountains into valleys, and over the waves — how immeasurably superior is such enjoyment to the admiration of the best imitation of it with paints and brush upon a few feet of canvas!

It was something, too, upon arrival at the cottage on the hill, to forget the woolly heads, and the tawny, yellow, molasses-tinted faces of the hot plains below, and in the fresh air of the mountains to see the brown hair of the pretty wife of our host blowing away from her blue eyes, like sun-lit clouds chased over spots of clear sky. Here they lived all the year, and found their enjoyment in health and good air, and in the cultivation of the ground, upon which, in his leisure from business, Mr. Sonderburg employed himself, and had succeeded in producing peaches, strawberries, cherries, and all the vegetables of temperate climes. "Not that he cared for them," he said, "but *they made him think he was in Denmark.*"

Upon one of the three little hills of which I have spoken, there lived a man illustrious or notorious, as his friends or his enemies may estimate his character. Robinson, in his "History of the Chieftains of Mexico," published in 1848, devotes a large space to him, and sums up all with, "Such is Santa Anna, whether good or bad — what his country has made him. A chapter of his history has yet to be written, which will, perhaps, display him in yet more brilliant colors; or, it may be, record another reverse, from which he will be unable to recover himself." His unfortunate country, where anarchy has reigned more than rulers or people, has not been favorable to the growth of political virtue, if there is such a thing anywhere. Of the thirteen generals whose lives are sketched in the little book referred to, no one, unless it be Iturbide, seems to have been actuated by real principles of honor or honesty. Even he, like Cæsar, was ambitious, and, like him, was murdered by the friends who once cringed at his throne.

Another chapter, comprising a period of seventeen years, can be written in the history of Santa Anna, and it would tell of him in brilliant colors again and again; many times would it tell of reverses from which he has recovered, and it may close with one from which it would seem that he will be unable to recover himself. But he may yet emerge from his retirement; it is not too late for one more chapter to be written, that may display him in his most brilliant colors at his death.

When the French invaded Mexico, Santa Anna was sent into exile; and he had chosen St. Thomas for his place of retirement — for what possible reason no one can imagine. It was not because of its climate, which is bad; nor for its luxuries and gayeties, of which there are none; nor could it be from motives of economy, for he is rich, and is not niggardly. It was not because he was among friends, for he was sometimes hissed when he appeared in the streets. Seldom, however, does he leave his own grounds. It was said by the virtuous gentlemen in town, whose means are not adequate to wholesale licentiousness, that he had a harem; and it struck me that their hatred of him was partly made up of envy. I had a curiosity to see the man, and accordingly sent a servant with a note, saying that the captain of the American steamer just arrived would esteem it an honor to be received by His Excellency, and asking him at what hour he would be disengaged. To this I received a reply, couched in true Spanish courtesy of language. As translated, —

"December 12, 1864.

"DEAR SIR: In reply to your polite note of to-day, I have the pleasure to say that, recognizing your delicate attention, I shall have the greater satisfaction in seeing you in this (*your*) house, at five o'clock this afternoon.

"Without more particulars, I subscribe myself, attentively,

"Yours, faithfully, Q. B. S. M.,

"A. L. DE SANTA ANNA."

I accordingly presented myself, accompanied by one of our passengers, at the hour appointed, and was received by his secretary, in a well-furnished parlor of his modest, but large and commodious one-story house. In a few moments the general came in, walking so easily without the aid of a cane, that it was impossible to distinguish his natural from his artificial leg. His carriage was military and erect, and he had the appearance of excellent health and condition. He is rather over than under six feet in height, and does not stoop at all. He wore white pantaloons and a dress coat with brass buttons. Notwithstanding the extreme heat, he kept this buttoned nearly to the throat. He was neatly shaven, and evidently just from his toilet, where some rejuvenating compound had blackened his hair. His complexion is rather dark, his eye piercing, but kindly, and his mouth firmly compressed, but not stern. When in conversation, his features were animated, and even handsome. There was nothing in his physiognomy to indicate a tyrant, brute, or sensualist. He extended his hand with great cordiality, and, by his affable manner, caused us to feel so much at home that there was no barrier to conversation. This took an extensive range, commencing with affairs at home, which were introduced by giving him some papers with the latest news of the war. I must accuse him of a little disingenuousness, for he declined to converse in English, from alleged inability to speak the language; and thus forced me into Spanish, which I spoke very imperfectly indeed; but he was kind enough to utter his words slowly and distinctly, so that we might understand all that he said. Perhaps it was as well, for it placed the burden of the talk upon him, where we wished it to be.

"I am a poor exile," he said; "but from my little watch-tower of St. Thomas I look all around." Then, sweeping the horizon with his arm, and pointing to the north-west, he continued: "I see the people of your great republic. They were once my enemies. I wish now that, instead of fighting among themselves, they and we were united to drive European despotism away from America." And his clenched fist came down upon the table, so that the whole room rattled. His feelings were clearly with the North, and he believed that the North would be finally victorious, but that "the Union would not be restored. It would be subjugation under military despotism. Over there in Europe," he continued, as he pointed to the north-east, "I see them disputing, and fighting a little. That does not concern us. They fight about their eternal balance of power, which never stays balanced. Let the big dogs and little dogs fight. Down there in

South America, the Spaniards and Peruvians are quarrelling. It will not amount to much. It will soon be settled." And then he reverted to Mexico, discoursing with mingled sadness and humorous irony upon the condition of affairs there. He looked upon the Austro-French empire as a very temporary affair. He described his ejection most amusingly. "Those French are a very polite people," said he; "very polite indeed. We talk, you know, of everything '*a su disposicion*' to our friends, but we don't mean that literally. They do. That Bazaine told me that a sea voyage would conduce to my health, and he furnished me with a steamer. He told me to go where I pleased, but not to come back to Mexico. That was the only condition the pleasant fellow made. Look here," he added, his voice, face, manner, everything changing him to another man, "*perhaps I may yet have the opportunity of reciprocating such attentions!*"

Perhaps he will reciprocate. Revolutions are no new things in Mexico. "Another chapter has yet to be written." Santa Anna is not yet too old for the battle of life. His sixty-five years sit lightly upon him, and with his wooden leg he may yet dance over the graves of his enemies. I have nothing to say of the character of Santa Anna. There are better and worse men than he, undoubtedly; but he is a pleasant gentleman, and I thank him for his kind reception, and for two hours of his agreeable conversation, although I felt a little vexed when I heard afterwards that he understood English perfectly well.

CHAPTER III.

Trade at St. Thomas. — Departure on the Voyage. — Passing the Islands. — Ocean Currents. — Crossing the Equator. — Visit from Neptune. — The South American Coast. — Arrival at Pernambuco. — Pleasant Surprise. — Passage to Rio de Janeiro. — Sale of the Steamer. — Change of Flags.

WHEN the steamers from Europe, Laguayra, and Havana meet here, as they sometimes do, St. Thomas is quite gay. The news which they bring seems to be of immense importance to everybody. The little six-by-four newspaper comes out extra, and the hotels, two of which are very good and well kept, reap of the harvest. By the establishment of merely nominal duties and slight *entrepôt* charges, Denmark has made this island the commercial exchange of the West Indies. Upon the true principle of small profits and large business she has acted, and thus made St. Thomas a much more profitable colony than when it was at the height of its agricultural prosperity. At this time, shortly preceding the Christmas holidays, there were swarms of traders, mostly Jews, who had come from all the leeward Islands, Venezuela, and

Mexico, to make their purchases. There is no better proof that all European merchandise can be afforded cheaper here than anywhere else; and the importance of steam communication with the United States is clearly demonstrated. English, Spanish, and an incomprehensible negro *patois* are the languages spoken. The governor, the three officers and seventy soldiers (who compose the army), and the collector of customs, speak Danish.

Having received on board all the coal required, we left St. Thomas on the 16th of December, to continue our voyage. The trade-wind from the eastward was very fresh, and the ship, being deeply loaded, made but slow progress at first. She was very wet and uncomfortable. But the breeze soon moderated, and we steamed along through the Caribbean Sea, passing close to the southern shore of Martinique, leaving Santa Lucia on our starboard hand. Daylight afforded us a near and enchanting view of the well-cultivated valleys and extensive plantations of the first named island, which charmed still more by contrast with the jagged cliffs and the barren volcanic peaks of the latter. At night we passed Barbadoes, so near to the town of Bridgetown, that we could see the lights in the houses, and hear the music which the land breeze wafted off for our serenade. And then, for ten days, no more land.

We traversed the ocean in its most unfrequented expanse, for no sailing vessel can make headway against the powerful current which sweeps around Cape St. Roque, and rushes on till it reaches the Gulf of Mexico. The ocean is no unmoved body of water, whose only pastime it is to make its wild leaps in the storm, and rest from its sport, basking in the rays of the sun. It is full of mighty rivers in its length and breadth, some moving so slowly that the line of their watery banks is imperceptible. Others, like this broad equatorial stream, more rapid as its channel narrows at the eastern point of South America, and at different times the navigator's hope and fear, are distinctly marked. So is the river current, which, doubling the Cape of Good Hope, gives the Indian Ocean an outlet into the South Atlantic. More famous than all is the Gulf Stream, which carries the warm water of the tropics so rapidly along, that it cannot cool till the polar river plunges into it, bearing along its islands of ice. Then, from the banks of Newfoundland, the united stream is deflected to the south, until reaching the equator, it is joined by the now sluggish current from the Cape of Good Hope. Uniting with this, and impelled by the force of the unfailing trade-winds, the great river, in which we find ourselves, rolls on again towards the

American continent, and thus the circuit of the ocean streams is complete.

Approaching the South American shore, where the Amazon and the Orinoco pour their floods into the sea, we observed the discolored water before seeing the land. We passed through a fleet of logs and uprooted trees, and perceptibly experienced the force of the current which pushes the ocean from the coast. The salometer also indicated a greater freshness of the water, though this was not apparent to the taste.

On the evening of the 27th December we crossed the equator. Hints had been given, for some days before, that Neptune would pay the ship a visit, and that the customary ceremonies of the occasion might be expected. As these have been so often described, a repetition of particulars would be of little interest.

The divinity was personated by one of the stoutest seamen, who had got himself up admirably for the character, with a wig of Manila hemp, and a shaggy garment, which completely disguised him. Hailing the ship from under the bowsprit, he was invited to come on board. He accordingly marched aft with a pair of grains, which well represented a trident, in his hands, and accepted a chair and a glass of wine upon the quarter-deck. Having asked if I had any of his children on board, he received liberty to search for them. There was one cockney young gentleman from New York, who had been loud in his expressions of contempt for Neptune, or for what he might do. No barking cur, with a whip held over him, ever subsided quicker than did this doughty hero. He said no more about whipping Neptune, but meekly walked before the awful apparition to his barber's shop upon the forecastle. The sight of the tub of grease and the iron hoop made him tremble at the idea of such lathering and shaving, and he begged to be allowed to capitulate. This favor was accorded him, and he then took a malicious pleasure in witnessing the sufferings of those victims from among the crew who could not, like him, afford the means of escape.

This practice is very generally discontinued. It is true that it has sometimes been carried to an extreme of roughness; but, as ordinarily conducted, it has been a great source of amusement. The true reason for its rare occurrence is, that "the monarch of the peopled deck," having no more taste for youthful sport, considers every attempt at fun to be an infringement of discipline, and because a sailor is considered by him a brute, whose business it is to labor, and nothing else. Many captains never can be made to realize that "all work and no play makes Jack a dull boy." Such treatment as they too often receive causes sailors to seek for their only amusement on shore, where, when they "dance," they dearly "pay the fiddler."

In order to escape the course of the current, after crossing the mouth of the Amazon, we ran close in to the north shore of Brazil, and made the land a little to the eastward of Maranham. Thence coasting along shore, we had before our eyes a constant panorama of green lowlands, with a background of blue mountains. We could see the cocoanut groves and plantain trees which shaded the lazy little fishing villages, and occasionally the bare white walls of some oven-built town, such as those wherein the old Portuguese delighted to roast themselves. They built them because they had such at home; as the Dutch built Batavia in a swamp, and dug canals through it, because it therefore looked like home; as Englishmen stuff themselves with roast beef and porter under the tropics, because they do so at home.

As we rounded Cape St. Roque, giving it a wide berth on account of the reef, we saw numberless catamarans. These little rafts are constructed of logs lashed together, upon which the adventurous natives make long voyages along the coast, and often go far out of sight of land in search of fish. As the water is always awash over the logs, the crew of three or four men are perched up on what resemble counting-house stools, where at least the upper part of their bodies can be dry. Baskets for their fish and provisions are similarly slung out of harm's way. They carry a large lateen sail, and in the early morning, as they are seen coming out of the harbors, they appear like a flock of white gulls upon the water. Like them, too, they are shy, and will not allow any one to approach them. It is said that their dread of strange ships arises from the treatment they have sometimes received from the American whalers, who frequent this coast. These vessels, being in want of men, have been known to run down the little craft purposely, and then, under pretence of saving the crews, have kidnapped them and impressed them into their service.

On the last day of December, and of the year 1864, at ten o'clock A. M., we anchored off the city of Pernambuco. Our object was to obtain a supply of coal for ship's use, if it could be advantageously bought. The town and its surroundings make a very pretty appearance from the sea. As for what is within, we had little opportunity for observation. It was an intensely hot day, and when we landed it seemed like entering a furnace. It is a pleasant thing to meet a familiar face in a strange land; and thus, when an old acquaintance, now established in business here, welcomed us upon the wharf, the unexpectedness of the meeting enhanced our gratification. Finding that the ship drew too much water to come into the inner harbor, and that a long time would be occupied in coaling outside, we were obliged to forego our intention. So, after a visit of a few hours to Pernambuco, we proceeded on the same evening upon our voyage. While the purser was busy in the market, looking after fruit and vegetables, of which he procured an abundant supply, we employed the time in a drive to the country house of our friend. Those who live on the shore, and were never at sea, cannot realize the delight of that hour's drive, of the walk in the shady garden, and of the company of trees, fruits, and flowers. Look in your books. You will find all about Pernambuco—the number of its inhabitants, its trade, productions, climate. I know nothing of these excepting of the latter, which would have troubled Shadrach, Meshach, and Abednego. Notwithstanding that, we had a delightful time. Remembrances of it, with the delicious fruits, lasted us to Rio de Janeiro. Nor in the four days' passage, though the bouquets from the lovely little garden began to fade, did we forget, or shall we forget, the charming fragment of a *séjour* at Pernambuco.

From Pernambuco to Rio de Janeiro, the distance is about eleven hundred and fifty miles. The weather was fine, and nearly calm. Over the smooth sea we steamed rapidly along, and on the morning of the 5th of January passed under the high headland of Cape Frio, as the day broke, throwing its sunlight upon the naked peak of the Sugar Loaf, the square tower of the Gavia, the crested Corcovado, the pinnacle of Tijuca, and all the familiar mountain faces which stand there the sentinels of ages, looking down upon the loveliest expanse of water in the world — the bay of Rio de Janeiro!

There, at noon, we anchored; and thence, under the stars and stripes, the "Cotopaxi" never sailed again. She was sold to the Brazilian government.

Returning to the United States, we sailed again in the steamer "Tejuca," arriving in Brazil in the autumn of 1865. In accordance with the plan proposed, all the details of this ship's journal are omitted, as uninteresting, until the date at which the subsequent narrative begins.

CHAPTER IV.

Effect of the Telegraph. — Distant Places brought near. — Brazil still remote. — Increasing Interest in the Country. — Various Descriptions thereof. — Agassiz and Fletcher. — Origin of the present Work.

OUR estimates of distance have been greatly affected by the general introduction of the magnetic telegraph, by which not only the extremes of the largest empires, but even continents separated by oceans, are enabled to exchange instantaneous communication.

While London and San Francisco are thus made to seem within easy reach, Brazil, which occupies a large portion of our western continent, is yet, practically, as distant as the unfrequented islands of the Pacific, or the frozen regions of the polar latitudes.

It is true that a circuitous line of steam navigation to Rio de Janeiro has been recently established; but the voyages, though made with a certain degree of regularity, are not more rapid than those often accomplished by sailing vessels. The capital of Brazil is still four thousand eight hundred miles in distance, and one month in time, apart from New York.

Nevertheless, Brazil has latterly attracted no little attention in the United States. Scientifically it has been explored by the enthusiastic Agassiz; voluminously it has been described by the imaginative Fletcher, as seen through his glasses of *couleur de rose;* and alluringly it has been placed before the ruined South of our land, by speculators, who care not if the deluded emigrants are ruined again.

It may be that these few pages, written with no pretensions to scientific or literary merit, and with no view of gain from "magnificent grants," will be read because they are not many. Brevity is a recommendation to which, in this instance, a fair claim can be made.

My observations have not been so extensive as could be wished. Still, they are all that I have to offer. There are those who, by a long residence in Brazil, should be better qualified to advance opinions upon the religion, morality, and pursuits of the people; but, as has often been observed, writers who are disposed to be candid are sometimes totally at variance in their judgments, even with the same opportunities of life-long observation.

These are merely the notes of a captain of a steamer, trading on the coast of Brazil. They are not made up from books, but from such rambles about city and country as time and opportunity permitted, and from intercourse with all sorts and conditions of passengers, with whom it was my fortune to associate at sea.

The voyages between Rio de Janeiro and Santos, sometimes extending to Paranagua, were made between the months of January and September, 1866. It was not till May, however, that the idea occurred to me, that it might be useful to others, as well as pastime to myself, to commit these observations to paper.

It is thus that my journal commences somewhat abruptly.

CHAPTER V.

Climate of Rio de Janeiro. — Intense Heat of the Weather. — Trips to Santos. — The Sea Breeze. — Refreshing Change. — Beauty of the Coast. — Configuration of the Country. — Rivers of the Table Land. — Island of St. Sebastian. — A Terrestrial Paradise. — Dream-Land.

MAY 6, 1866. — At this season of the year, which should correspond with the November of northern latitudes, instead of the cooler weather we might reasonably expect after the terrific and unusual heat of the summer months, we are again dissolving. The heat in Rio de Janeiro is not to be measured by thermometers. Indeed, the mercury is seldom above 85° Fahrenheit; but there is a humidity in this heated atmosphere that kills all oxygen, and makes the air in and about the city more oppressive and exhausting than my experience can call to mind elsewhere, excepting in Algeria. There, the sirocco was wont to drive us to the stone floor of the bath-room, and leave us panting like the hart after the water-brook, till the three days' agony was over.

But the African sirocco is only an occasional

misery. Here, a similar heat has been constant, though less intense, with scarcely an interval since our arrival in December. Day after day has been a dog-day, as the murky, inactive clouds have hung over the city; and the nights, intolerable on shipboard or on shore, so far from bringing relief, have left us unresisting victims to those birds of prey that penetrated through the nets where air could scarcely enter. As a physician has truly said of this climate, the liver must inevitably suffer, for it is obliged to do double duty — for itself and for the lungs.

Our trips to Santos have afforded some relief to this lassitude and debility. The moment the bows of the ship looked beyond the "Sugar-loaf," an oppressive load was removed from the lungs and from the brain, and there was a day's vacation for exhausted nature.

If anything could be worse than the air of Rio de Janeiro, it was that of Santos; and we were rejoiced to leave that port again, so that in fact the only enjoyment we had, was at sea.

Added to the pure air of the ocean there was a superior mental tonic. We were exhilarated by the beautiful and picturesque scenery of the route, embracing a view of near and distant mountains, and of a coast lined alternately with sterile rocks, wild verdure, and cultivated soil. For this distance of two hundred miles, the character of the coast is peculiar to Brazil, excepting an occasional variety which enhances the charm of the general outline. The meadows from the border of the sea stretch back on a level for ten or fifteen miles, and then there is an abrupt, sometimes almost perpendicular rise to a height of three thousand feet, to what is called the "Serra." This level attained, the generally very even country is sometimes varied by little hills and valleys, never rising nor descending many feet, until it reaches the base of the Andes, on the western side of the continent.

Rivers flow sluggishly along this vast prairie — rivers that could be navigated by steamers, if they, like the salmon, could jump up thither from the ocean. Little do these lazy streams imagine what is before them, till, rolling along to the very brink of the Serra, they take their tremendous leaps; and, spreading themselves now into broad cascades, then into silver threads, and often into scarcely more than misty vapor, they tumble and dance over rocks, and half float in the air, till they find their level on the plains below, and there, gathering their scattered waters again, become rivers once more, and, as such, surrender themselves to the ocean.

The high and richly cultivated Island of St. Sebastian lay in our track, with a channel of one or two miles in width between it and the main land. Outside or inside, the distance was nearly the same; but, whenever daylight permitted, it was our favorite enjoyment to pass through the narrow inland passage. Excepting the Bosphorus, there is nothing in my memory that equals these shores in loveliness. In some respects this strait is even superior to the Bosphorus, though the latter is adorned by palaces and kiosks, which are wanting here. But for these we have a compensation in the deep, unfading green of the tropics, and the innumerable cascades which sparkle with silver threads upon the upper rocks. The table-land on the summit of the island seems to hold a perpetual reservoir of water, and every plantation and garden on the slope has its own little river or brook. Pretty, too, in the distance, — and it is only in the distance that Turkish or Brazilian towns are pretty, — are the little villages which hang upon the hills, and the abodes of the fishermen upon the shores.

The island always seemed to us to be a sort of dream-land, for there was never a sign of life upon it. We passed close to the banks of the channel, fired guns, and blew the shrill steam-whistle; but the only response was the echo from the hills. Everything was silent, and we wondered how the little brooks dared to roll over the stones. No one appeared to work or to be active in these pleasure-grounds of the Castle of Indolence. Even the fishermen seemed to have no lines, as they leaned dreamily over the sides of their canoes, and they would scarcely have moved a paddle to save themselves from destruction. They were all Brazilians on St. Sebastian, and God treats them as He treats the lilies of the field — He lets them grow and thrive.

CHAPTER VI.

Santos. — A quiet City. — Noise banished. — Advantages unimproved. — Impediments to Commerce. — Brazilian Want of System. — Swarms of Office-holders. — Bribery and Corruption. — Incessant Rains. — A Dutchman in Despair.

SANTOS is approached by first passing a rocky islet, whereon is a lighthouse, and where, in former days, was a semaphoric telegraph station. For some reason, notwithstanding that trade has increased, the telegraph has been discontinued. Many things march backward in Brazil, and among the people there is a great dread of improvement. We were accustomed to fire a gun on our arrival in the river; but we were notified not to do so again, under penalty of a fine, because it awoke those who were taking their siesta. On the last 4th of July, the American admiral, wishing to celebrate the day by saluting at every port on his station, ordered the United States store-ship "Onward" to Santos for this express purpose. The commander was waited upon by the authorities, and at their earnest solicitation he consented not to make a noise.

After rounding the lighthouse island, we enter a

magnificent bay, at the head of which is a hard beach, circling around for miles. Its upper limit is fringed by low woods, from which peep out white "chacaras," or country seats, surrounded by pretty gardens. These are the summer residences of the wealthier inhabitants, and, as it seemed to us, the only comfortable abodes for anybody, either in summer or in winter; for the houses in the town are the opposites of all our ideas of dwelling-places, so small, damp, and cheerless do they appear.

Beyond the eastern end of the beach, across the river, is the fort, which nominally defends the harbor. This work is an antiquated Portuguese pile of brick and mortar, which in its best days would scarcely have withstood musketry, and is now, of course, useless for defence. The river is a narrow stream, not more than a quarter of a mile in width, but of sufficient depth for the largest class of ships. It winds prettily through a low plain, covered with forest and guava trees, till the town of Santos is reached, at a distance of seven miles from the fort.

Nature has here supplied every convenience for commerce, such as a civilized people would gladly accept and improve. In our turn, when it came, the steamer was visited, entered, and at last permitted to discharge; and this discharging must needs be done at the custom-house wharf, — a privilege which likewise came in turn, and was of course very uncertain.

I have said that Brazil steps backward; and she is doing this while she professes a wish to "open trade and to encourage immigration." Let us take our own case as an illustration of the way in which she will be likely to accomplish these objects. On a coastwise route like this, of two hundred miles, in the United States, we could have made the round trip at least eight times monthly, receiving and discharging full cargoes. Here, owing to no other cause than the vexatious impediments offered by the government, we could scarcely make three trips in that time. In the first place, the custom-house is closed on all holidays and saints' days; and there are holidays many, and of saints' days an unknown number, which is continually increasing. By and bye, when there come to be more than three hundred and sixty-five of them in the calendar, the days must be divided, one saint taking the morning and another the evening. As it is now, the festival days only occupy about half the time. On these days no business is done. On the secular days the custom-house hours, within which ships are permitted to load and discharge, are included between seven A. M. and four P. M., out of which one hour is taken for breakfast and two hours for dinner. However active a crew may be, they are obliged to conform to the slow movements of the custom-house employees, who make a pretence of working at the same time.

After the loading is completed, there generally follows a day's work to clear at the custom-house. Thence, after signing a multiplicity of documents, — I counted them once; there were ninety-six, — the captain is at length released. After being visited by health-boat, police-boat, and guard-boat, we finally proceed to sea. When we enter port at the other end of our route, the same ceremonies are again to be observed; and if the boarding officials are at breakfast, we may remain at anchor two or three hours blowing off steam, until their convenience is suited. And all this nonsense, be it remembered, applies not only to foreign trade, but more especially to the coasting trade, which Brazil has so recently thrown open to all nations. As I was the first to take advantage of the permission, and have followed the business for nearly a year, I feel competent to assure others that, with all the annoyances and the small profits, *le jeu ne vaut pas la chandelle.*

There is no true idea of system or order among the Brazilians, at least in public affairs. The post-office is quite as badly administered as the custom-house. There is no certainty whatever that your letters will be despatched, or that your correspondence from home will reach you. There is a chance of success, and that is all. Bushels of letters are scattered about in the post-office of Rio de Janeiro. You are invited to enter and help yourself; and it may readily be supposed that in this way some people find the letters of others, if they cannot find any of their own. Some years ago, when Mr. Gordon, who had previously filled the office of postmaster in Boston, was consul here, he offered to place the Brazilian post-office upon an American footing, saving, it is to be hoped, the bad feature of rotation in office. His well-meant proposal was declined. Like the Chinese, the Brazilians cling to "olo cussum;" and it is a very peculiar old custom that in part accounts for the vexations of which we complain.

In England and in the United States the relation of "godfather," although nominally a very responsible trust, is generally a sinecure. There is a promise that the child, whose parents thus pay a sort of compliment to the person who acts as sponsor, shall be religiously educated, and shall say his Catechism like a good boy, which promise the godfather proposes to trouble himself very little in keeping. In Brazil this ceremony means a very different thing. The rich and influential are begged to assume the honor, and can seldom refuse to take upon themselves this obligation for their poor relations. They make all sorts of religious promises; but these are interpreted to mean a care for the child's advancement in this life. As the godfather naturally wishes to accomplish his vows with as little expense to himself as possible, what better can he do than to provide the young man, as soon as he is of suitable age, with an office under the government? And if government has not a sufficient number of offices at its disposal, how can the influence of the Duke, Marquis, Baron, or Comendador be retained more easily than by creating new offices for new office-holders? Thus these men in office go on and multiply, till the cap-bands and stripes are becoming so numerous that the people will soon be like the company of a down-east schooner — captain, mate, cook, and no crew. And so the system becomes not only an expensive arrangement for the Brazilians themselves, but likewise a burden and an intolerable nuisance to foreigners, and a serious impediment in the way of commerce.

Moreover, it may be readily seen that where so many are feeding from the public crib, there must be a scarcity of fodder for all. Hence proceed bribery and corruption, according to the scale of office, mounting upwards from a milreas to the colossal figure sometimes reached at Washington.

The city of Santos is the principal seaport of the province of San Paulo. It was settled at a very early period in the history of the country, by the Portuguese, who were at no loss to perceive the advantages of its situation for commercial purposes; and these are all the advantages to which it could ever lay claim. Nothing but the love of money could entice one to live there. It lies on a low, alluvial soil, half the time submerged, — so that walking is impracticable, — and, for a portion of almost every day, is deluged by torrents of rain, which cease for an hour or two only. Then comes forth, in this brief interval, a burning sun, to exhale the moisture from the spongy ground, and to pour down a heat which renders the stifling air little better than the fumes from a charcoal furnace.

I could fully credit the story told of a Dutch captain, whose race is generally so phlegmatic. His vessel was chartered to load a cargo of coffee, and a certain number of "working days" were stipulated for, "rainy days not included." It did not suit the convenience of the merchant to ship the cargo until the price had fallen, which time seemed afar off. And so the honest Dutchman remained at his anchor day after day, week after week, and month after month; for it rained so often that scarcely a day could be counted against the inexorable coffee-dealer. At length the skipper's pipe and his patience gave out together, and he became raving mad. There was time to obtain a new captain from Amsterdam, it is said, before coffee fell and the rain ceased to fall.

CHAPTER VII.

A Decayed Town. — Brighter Prospects. — Cultivation of Cotton in Brazil. — Advantages therefor over the United States. — Mutations in Planting. — Cotton, Coffee, Sugar. — Opportunities to make a Fortune. — Primitive Modes of Conveyance. — Mules and Muleteers. — Cruelty to Animals.

SANTOS, with its decayed landing-places and dilapidated warehouses, reminds one of Newburyport, Salem, and other such towns at home, that were once busy commercial marts, but have long since lost their trade, and have become neglected and forlorn. But now it would seem that a new and brighter era may dawn upon the city of Santos. Wherever in the world cotton can be grown, its cultivation has received an impetus from the late American civil war. Various nations have begun to compete for the cheapest production of this absolutely necessary staple, and none have a fairer chance of success, in building their fortunes upon our ruin, than Brazil, if her people can display sufficient energy. The most sanguine planters scarcely hoped to do more than to make large profits while the war continued; but they now see an unlimited future of prosperity before them. They are quite sure that the labor system of the Southern States will be much more expensive than heretofore, and that this climate, even with free labor, which all anticipate eventually, will give them every advantage over us. Their reasoning is simple, and not easily refuted.

For example, in the province of San Paulo, of which Santos is the seaport, there is no winter, properly so called, although it is within the limits of the southern temperate zone. Something is produced from the soil, in alternate crops throughout the year, and there are generally two crops of cotton annually, or, at least, three crops in two years. There is no season in which the laborer need remain idle. He can always be producing something for his employer or for himself. In either case it is the same, for it enters into the cost of raising cotton, as the price of remunerative labor. Nor, like the southern negro, whose service cannot be made available in the winter, does the laborer here require warm clothing, if any at all; for clothing is a luxury indulged in only on Sundays and holidays. Slave labor, or free labor, is, then, undeniably cheaper here. Moreover, the expense of cultivation is infinitely less with the proper tools, of which the Brazilians are so slow to learn the use. Cotton with us is planted yearly. Here the plants last from five to seven years without renewal.

When slavery existed in the United States, cotton could be raised for seven cents per pound; and then Cotton *was* King. What a fall he has had from his throne, dragging down his ministers and his immediate vassals with him, involving in the ruin those who were obliged to dethrone him! The kingdom of Cotton is changed into a world-wide republic. Many nations will be the gainers, while we are losers. At this time, with our present transition of labor systems, it is estimated that cotton cannot be raised for less than twenty cents per pound. Doubtless, in the course of years, either by the utilization of black labor, which the hopes of some anticipate, or by the influx of emigrants, this condition will be improved. But, meanwhile, the outside world will get a prodigious start; and it is difficult to conceive, that, with all the appliances we can bring to bear, we can reduce the present cost of production one half — to ten cents. To this must be added the internal revenue tax of three cents, and the export duty, if our government is so unwise as to place any further restrictions upon industry.

In this district of San Paulo, cotton can be raised for very little more than our present revenue tax and the proposed export duty; and this even with the antiquated tools and the slow energies of Brazilians. In many parts of the empire the experiment has proved unsuccessful. Especially is this true of the country near Rio de Janeiro, where the plant is often utterly destroyed by worms.

I know an American gentleman in charge of a large fazenda a few leagues from that city, who has lost his entire crop for the three years since he commenced planting, and whose almost indomitable perseverance has been at last forced to succumb. He is now successfully cultivating sugar-cane. Sugar was formerly the chief product of the district of San Paulo. It was abandoned some years ago, when the world's demand for coffee suddenly became so great; and then the cane-fields became green with the beautiful coffee tree. At present there is not sugar enough made here to supply the wants of a single village. It formed the bulk of our cargoes from Rio de Janeiro, whence it is reëxported, after being landed from Bahia and Pernambuco.

Now, in their turn, the coffee trees in San Paulo are neglected, and the fields are white with cotton, destined to occupy the ground, at least for some years, until some other great change comes over the wants of the world.

With this prospect in view there is a splendid future for the city of Santos. Already a direct trade is opened between that city and Liverpool by the screw steamers, which touch monthly on their route to and from Montevideo. All that is wanted is energy. For

Americans, if there are any who can endure the detestable climate, there are sure opportunities offered for amassing wealth.

This city has scarcely more than four thousand inhabitants, its population having decreased within a few years. The price of land and other real estate is just now very low. Emigrants will find it advantageous to settle near the seaboard, rather than in the interior, whence it is so expensive to bring produce to market. This has hitherto been brought for hundreds of miles on the backs of mules. It is still necessarily thus transported to the city of San Paulo, distant from Santos about forty-five miles by the railroad just completed. So slow are the Brazilians to see the advantages of this mode of conveyance, that most of them still adhere to the old method of carriage for the whole distance.

Every mule brings on his back two bags of coffee or two bales of cotton. The bags of coffee each weigh one hundred and twenty-eight pounds, and the bales of cotton one hundred and twelve pounds. They make long and slow journeys, averaging about sixteen miles per day.

The entrance of a "troop" of mules into the city is a lively sight. They are always preceded by a white horse, with a string of bells upon his neck, all the mules obediently following this leader. Sometimes troops of several hundreds arrive on a morning; and again there are days with no arrivals. Most of the muleteers are rough, shaggy Western islanders, or half Indians. They are finely formed men, with handsome features, but a devilish expression — such as one would prefer to meet in town by daylight, rather than on the mountains by night. When the pack-saddles are taken off, the mules are pitiable objects. The continual sawing of their loads for a long journey of hundreds of miles not only abrades the skin, but grinds off the raw flesh down to the very bones. It is hard to imagine that self-interest, to say nothing of humanity, can permit such cruelty.

CHAPTER VIII.

Railroads in Brazil. — Natural Obstacles Encountered. — Dom Pedro Segundo Railroad. — A Stupendous Work. — Excursion by Rail to San Paulo. — Precipitous Grades. — Frightful Chasms. — Queer Sensations. — Aspects of Nature in the North and South. — City of San Paulo. — Institutions of Education. — Return to the Plains, &c.

AT last that inevitable institution, the railroad, has found its way to Brazil, as it will, doubtless, one of these days, reach Timbuctoo. In no country has it more natural obstacles to contend against than here. There are several small railroads in the northern provinces, running on levels, a few miles from the cities; but there, and at Rio de Janeiro, they have, until lately, been content to stop without any effort to overcome the hills.

The first great work undertaken — and it is really a stupendous work — was the Dom Pedro II. Railroad. By the aid of English capital, and the skill of American engineers, — the Messrs. Ellison, who should be held in everlasting remembrance here, — this road has already been carried one hundred and twenty miles into the interior from Rio de Janeiro. A way has been found to climb precipices; bridges have been thrown over deep chasms, and solid mountains have been tunnelled, in one instance for the distance of two miles. No better masonry can be seen in the world; and it is admitted by Europeans and Americans who have passed over this line, and are qualified to judge of it in comparison with others, that it is a most complete triumph of engineering art.

Another road is just completed, — the one already referred to, between Santos and San Paulo, — which will do a vast deal to open trade, and will save the back of many a poor mule. It is to be continued farther inland; and mules, if they could pray, — and their prayers would have a better chance of being heard than those of their drivers, — should pray for its speedy extension.

The road is scarcely yet in running order; but as we were desirous of seeing a work which has been so much lauded, and also of visiting the city of San Paulo, we accepted the invitation of the superintendent to go over the route. Owing to its unfinished condition, we could have accomplished the distance much more speedily and pleasantly by diligence, or on horseback, by a good mountain road; but we should not have seen what we did see under some difficulties. The connections were intended to have been made; but unfortunately they were not made, so that we were thirty hours in accomplishing our forty-five miles. We thus made a speed, including stops, of one and a half mile per hour, which rate it is intended to increase by and bye.

Our first stopping-place was Mugi, a village fifteen miles from Santos, and at the end of the low level. Making a virtue of necessity, we passed a very pleasant afternoon and night at this collection of *adobe* huts.

At such places, the "*vendas*," or grog-shops, generally do duty as hotels; but here a German landlord has established himself, and really keeps a very comfortable inn. His chief customers are the English employees of the road, from whom he makes no little profit on beer and brandy. Mr. Sharp, the contractor, has a good two-story dwelling-house, which is surrounded by quite a little settlement of his countrymen. The aristocracy consist of Mr. Sharp and a Scotch doctor and his family. The plebeians are the engine-drivers and understrappers. Glad enough to hear our own language spoken, we accommodated ourselves to both extremes of society, and thus whiled away our time as best we might.

In the morning we recommenced our journey by being drawn up the inclined plane to the "Alto," or top of the Serra, which is twenty-seven hundred feet above Mugi. This part of the trip is a pleasure which, taken once in a man's life, is, as a pleasure, sufficient. The grade is one foot in ten, and the ascent is effected by stationary engines, four of which are placed at nearly equal distances apart. A large wire rope is attached to the train, when the invisible power, a mile above, commences operations. Slowly we begin to move upwards on the track, which winds along the brink of an ever-growing precipice.

Uncomfortable is a very mild word to apply to the sensation produced; and, as we go up, up, up, this feeling naturally increases — a possible fall being calculated to be more and more like annihilation in proportion to the ascent gained. These queer sensations arrive at their greatest intensity on the last stretch, when, looking from the window, we perceive a chasm yawning beneath, the remembrance of which makes my pen quiver even now.

It is admitted that the road is dangerous. And thus it will continue to be for some time, at least until the banks settle so that they will not be washed away, as they frequently are now, by the heavy rains. Fortunately the "slides" have taken place when no train was upon the track; but this immunity cannot always be counted upon. A passenger must have the unpleasant reflection that he may be called upon to "assist" at the first fatal catastrophe.

But all these perils — at least for those who have never made the ascent before — are more than counterbalanced by the exhilaration of the mountain air, and by the wonderful magnificence and beauty of the scenery. The fields below "stand dressed in living green;" the mountain-tops, the hill-sides, and the valleys are all alike of this color, in different shades of their own verdure, and all perpetually changing, as the dark or fleecy clouds throw their shadows over the scene. Even the rocky cliffs and precipices, steep down for hundreds and even thousands of feet, scarcely show their barrenness, being covered, as are also the forest trees, with thick-hanging parasitic flowers. All else that Nature deigns to wear to vary and display more forcibly her everlasting mantle of green, are the silver-white ribbons of the streams, which scatter themselves far and wide over the slopes, and add another charm to what would already seem perfection.

There are landings on this great staircase, which we ascended, where the cars are attached to the engines above. Each of these engines turns a shaft, around which is wound the wire cable, that draws up one train while it gently lowers another. These "down trains" are not absolutely necessary, but when convenient they are used as aids to the engines.

Just before we reached the summit, heavy clouds

began to gather around us; and when we arrived at the "Alto" it was in the midst of a pouring rain, while everything below was smiling in sunshine. And now came the "winter of our discontent," for again there was no connection of trains; and in default of it there were no pretty Scotch girls, as at Mugi, to dispel the dreariness of the day before us. So we crept into a miserable *venda;* and there, in a miscellaneous company, listening to all sorts of oaths and jargon, breathing the aroma of caxache rum, garlic, unwashed Portuguese, undressed negroes, and the general stench of humidity, we waited till evening, when the train arrived.

As the afternoon advanced, the mist cleared away; and when we were at length upon our road to San Paulo, it was that beautiful hour when daylight dies, and when the shadows of night are seen creeping along to its funeral. The change was scarcely perceptible, so nearly alike were the half-clear daylight and the night illumined by stars. Our eyes revelled in perfection when the moon rose, far away beyond the vast plains, over which we were so rapidly whirled. Thanks to those powerful engines, we had been elevated into another atmosphere — a different world! Below, in Santos and on the plains we had left, the "pale moon, with sickly ray," was scarcely penetrating the miasmatic fog, and the stars were glimmering like lights from the attic windows of some pest-visited city. Here, all bright and clear, the night-lights of heaven danced through an air which was the breath of electric life. It was like the glowing October of Vermont. What a month that is! And how faint and feeble, in comparison, was this scene, that reminded us of it! There is no such pure atmosphere, no such variety of view, and, above all, no such fresh coloring, in the tropics as in our northern climes. Here we pass through immense tracts of wild woods, where the trees of perennial green are giant garden plants, blooming with flowers. We cannot but love and caress Nature, as, thus gaudily dressed, she is forever smiling upon us; but she is like the women of this clime — lovely, languid, inexpressive, always the same.

In these regions, Nature, animate or inanimate, is alike lazy, — almost too lazy to die as she dies with us, only to live again, — throwing around herself such a pall of beauty, that, when we look upon her autumn, the idea of our own death is robbed of its terrors.

Yet this was a near approach to a temperate climate; and the contrast with the deadly, sickening heat we had so long endured was so great, that the sensations caused by unaccustomed pulsation were for a time almost uncomfortable.

The country through which we passed was generally

level, and partially cleared, affording, one would think, excellent pasturage, and good land for growing wheat or corn. And yet no cattle are raised near the coast, no butter or cheese is made, no wheat is grown, and Indian corn is not produced in sufficient quantity for home consumption. The reasons assigned are, that cattle can be had for almost nothing far in the interior. So they are driven down to the sea, and what the flies and the "bichos" leave is consumed by the people. They are grateful that these destroyers cannot eat the hide and the bones, which are nearly all that is left. As for wheat and Indian corn, they say there is more profit in raising coffee and cotton, and they can better import these grains than raise them. They obtain very good fresh cheese from the province of Minas; and they rather prefer the butter which has become rancid, when imported from Europe or the United States, high as the price is compared with what they could afford it for themselves, — for a Brazilian is as fond of grease as a Russian.

The people here all believe that milk is an unwholesome article of food. It is a fact that two cows supply the whole city of Santos. Every morning these, and these only, may be seen driven about the town, each with her muzzled calf tied to the end of her tail. The milk is drawn off at the doors of those who require it, the procession of cow, calf, and milkman passing through whole streets without a call. When a customer is found, he is fully supplied from a small measure containing less than half a pint.

At a late hour of the evening we were landed at the station, which is in the outskirts of the city of San Paulo. Thence we walked to the Hôtel d'Europe, through clean, well-paved streets, bordered with low houses, neat, at least outwardly.

In almost every foreign place we have found a "Hôtel d'Europe;" and as it has so often happened to be the best in the town, we decided to trust ourselves to it here. Nor were we mistaken or disappointed. The hotel compared favorably with any yet seen in Brazil, and was superior to those of the capital. The table was good and abundant, and the price for transient guests was only three milreas (one dollar and fifty cents) per day, including *vin ordinaire*. In a French hotel, by the by, this is indispensable. Were Frenchmen on a wreck with an allowance of a crumb of bread and a drop of water, they would expect the *vin ordinaire* to be included. Fruit was abundant here, the strawberries and grapes being particularly fine. I believe that cherries are unknown in Brazil. We were told, by an English resident, that the peaches, in their season, are equal to those of New Jersey; but when he added, "They are not hup to those we have in Hingland," we knew that he was not qualified to make the comparison.

The city of San Paulo contains twenty thousand inhabitants, and has a great deal of trade with the interior. For the present the terminus of the railroad is here, and thus for some time San Paulo will be the depot of all the merchandise going to and from the seaboard. But when the road is opened, as it soon will be, into the rich district of Campinas, this place will lose its commercial importance. Railroads terminating in small villages sometimes convert them into great cities; by passing through large towns they often cause them to dwindle down to small villages.

The people of this province are called Paulistas. They are generally of a purer race than their more northern countrymen, having less negro blood in their veins; nor are they so much mixed with the Indians as the inhabitants south, in Paranagua. The women are often pretty, and not unfrequently of fair, clear complexion, through which blushes, unknown elsewhere, may occasionally be seen. Well located in San Paulo are the chief literary institutions of the empire. It enjoys the finest climate in Brazil, and surely pure air enters into the production of clear brains. The course of education in law, physic, and divinity is very complete, occupying terms of seven years. It was vacation time, and the three classes of students, who form a lively and important part of the population, being away at their homes, the town was considered dull. These young men, belonging almost always to the richest families of the empire, disburse a great deal of money among the Paulistas, who are consoled in their absence by the reflection that when they return they will bring with them all the money that can be wrung out of their "governors." It being therefore "the dull season," we could please ourselves only with viewing the outside of the college buildings.

We had no letters of introduction, and so we made no acquaintances, excepting those of our very civil landlord and of an American dentist — for American dentists find employment in all Brazilian towns, and in the mouths of almost all Brazilian women who can afford to avail themselves of their services. Pleased with what we had seen, and invigorated by our short sojourn in these upper regions, we trusted ourselves again to the wire rope, and were lowered down to the hot plains below. Soon again we found ourselves on the deck of the steamer, and on the next day sailed for Rio de Janeiro.

CHAPTER IX.

Trip on the Dom Pedro Segundo Railroad. — American and English Engineering Compared. — Dismal Swamp. — Terminus of the Road. — Future Extension. — A Negro-loving Philanthropist. — Laziness and Cunning of the Negroes. — Unprofitable Servants. — The Plan a Failure.

BY invitation of Mr. Ellison, engineer-in-chief of the Dom Pedro II. Railroad, we had a favorable opportunity of travelling over this magnificent work to its present terminus, one hundred and twenty miles from Rio de Janeiro. We could not avoid comparing it very favorably with the San Paulo road, and feeling pride that the American style of construction was, at least in this one instance, so immeasurably superior to the English.

This road follows for a greater distance the low level, which on this part of the coast extends about forty miles before the inevitable Serra is reached. The Serra, or upper platform of land, may average three thousand feet high for its whole extent. For the first ten miles the road passes through the beautiful and highly cultivated suburbs of the city, leaving on

the right, the palace and grounds of San Christovão, and cutting through the gardens of the numerous chacaras inhabited by the wealthy citizens. For the rest of the level, as far as Belem, at the foot of the Serra, the land is divided about equally between plantation, pasturage, and morass, with here and there a village at the railway stations. The cars are mostly of the American pattern, which is generally preferred in this warm climate.

For ten miles before arriving at Belem (or Bethlehem), we passed through a most dismal swamp, indeed. The waste of human life in the construction of this short section was horrible, and the few laborers and overseers who survived the inevitable fever of this pool of abominations, are now tottering to the grave with ruined constitutions.

We had no such discomforts here as on the San Paulo road. Although the rise from the coast to the Serra is the same in both places, we were not obliged to change seats or to feel that our lives hung by a thread, or even by a wire rope. Notwithstanding that in some places the grade could not be reduced to less than one foot in fifteen, the stalwart American iron horse jogged along, slowly, it is true, and straining his muscles to the utmost, but carrying us bravely through the notches and along the sides of the hills. There was a feeling of perfect security as we surveyed the solid masonry and stone walls—seemingly as durable as those of the Simplon, or of the road over Mount Cenis. We could not but marvel that Americans should have so far surpassed in a foreign land anything that has been done at home.

The scenery is of the same character as that of the Serra farther south, but more beautiful in variety. Lost for a moment in wonder at the giant forest which surrounded us, the next instant opened a vista through which we looked far down on the valley of Macacos, extending for miles between two spurs of the Serra—every foot of it a fruitful garden.

Rhodeo is the first station, about sixty miles from Rio de Janeiro, and nearly at the "Alto" of the Serra. From thence, after rising three hundred feet more, until a height of three thousand feet is attained, there is a more gradual descent to the valley and river of Parahiba, where is the present terminus of the road for traffic. It is partially completed, and will soon be opened as far as Entre Rios, where it crosses the celebrated "União e Industria" carriage road. For some forty miles across the valley the grade is comparatively level, and there are few natural obstacles to be overcome

But the march of the Dom Pedro II. Railroad is onward. Its future progress is over and through mountains and rocks, till the great mining district of

Minas, now the journey of weeks, is brought within two days' communication with the capital. Government cannot well spare the money, depleted as the treasury now is by an unprofitable war; but as it has assumed the responsibility of finishing the road, it will be done. The investment will, at all events, prove a better one than that in Paraguay, where life, as well as treasure, has been so uselessly sacrificed.

Returning towards the city, and passing Rhodeo, we were landed, by the kind invitation of Dr. Gunning, at the platform a few steps from his chacara. Charming as is this beautiful retreat, perched in the mountain wilderness, looking through its clearings down on the lovely valley of Macacos, there is something more charming in the character of our amiable hosts.

Dr. Gunning is a *practical* negro-loving philanthropist. Although his schemes have been failures, and his efforts for the improvement of the black race have been entirely without success, he is yet as sanguine as ever, still persevering, in spite of misfortune, and even of ridicule, so much harder to bear.

Coming as we did from a country where we knew too well how much of the pretended love for the negro has emanated from that political ambition which has made him the mere tool for the purposes of party and of power, we could not but admire and love this disinterested enthusiast.

Dr. Gunning left a high position in the Medical College of Edinburgh, sixteen years ago, and came to Brazil for the improvement of his health. Here, in a short time, his skill as a physician, and some profitable investments in the mines, secured him an ample fortune. Had his constitution permitted him to return to England, he would, doubtless, have found full scope for his benevolence among the poor whites there; but as he was obliged to remain in Brazil, he naturally turned his attention to the prevailing color. In short, as an individual, he resolved to devote his time, talents, and property to the experiment which nations have tried in vain. He would raise the black to the level of the white race, by a practical trial of a theory not new, but variously attempted — that of "giving the black man a fair chance."

With this object steadily in view, he purchased some thirty-five or forty negroes. He bought a tract of land nearly two miles square on the railroad which was then building, about six years ago, and on it the pretty cottage at which we were so hospitably entertained now stands.

In its neighborhood he built comfortable huts for his negroes, and gave to each as large a garden spot as he required. At that time the planters and other slave-owners were gaining enormously by the labor of their negroes upon the railroad, so that the value of a slave was soon cleared. The good doctor asked himself the question, "If a planter can clear a negro, why cannot a negro clear himself?" A woman's answer, "Because —" would have been more to the purpose than his own. At any rate, the negroes did not clear themselves, and they remain on hand to this day.

The doctor commenced a perfect system of book-keeping. Each colored gentleman had his name at the head of a page, with Dr. on the left and Cr. on the right: Dr. to his first cost, interest on the same, and subsequent expenses for food, clothing, &c.; Cr. by cash received for his individual labor. When the accounts balanced he was to be free. But none of the accounts ever came to be balanced.

The negro is often not so much of a fool as his white apologist. He would have no objection to freedom if it could be had for nothing, for the days of idleness before him are a tempting luxury. But these fellows had the sense to see that with such a master as Dr. Gunning, freedom would not be worth working for. The result was, that they were nearly half the time drunk, or sick in the hospital, and when they did work, they worked so unprofitably that the railroad company dispensed with their services.

The doctor is now using them in clearing and planting his own grounds, and crediting them with their daily labor. In this way he promises himself that they will eventually earn their freedom. His neighbors say that the work would be done in a cheaper and better manner if he gave them their freedom at once, and then hired the slaves of others.

In the mean time the doctor submits quietly to the robbery of his hen-roosts, the stealing of his fruit and vegetables, the surreptitious milking of his cows, and the other annoyances, great and small, which the presence of these vagabonds entails upon him. His corn is gathered early, but it is not gathered for him; and his crop of green coffee is large for others, while that of ripe coffee is small for himself. The black lilies "toil not, neither do they spin," and the slaves are hard masters, "reaping where they have not sown."

When our excellent friend first made his investment, he was very inconsiderate in the explanation of his plans to the negroes. One morning after instructing them in the mysteries of book-keeping, he added that, in case of his death at any time, they would be free at once. On the same night he was attacked in his bed by a negro with an iron bar, and seriously beaten over the head. Fortunately the generous Scotchman's head was harder than his heart, and the only result of the blow was an enlargement of the organ of caution.

CHAPTER X.

A Brazilian Plantation under Yankee Management. — Description of the Fazenda. — Sunshine and Shade. — Brazilian Cookery. — Ride over the Estate. — Working of the Negroes. — Freedom and Slavery. — Comparative Advantages and Disadvantages. — Moral Reflections, &c.

THERE is a fazenda on the line of the railroad, about twenty miles from Rio de Janeiro, which belonged to a Portuguese family for many generations. At last the family decayed, and the plantation likewise went to ruin. The old stone buildings began to crumble, and the brush-wood, starting up in the place of neglected sugar-cane, soon became a young forest, where the cattle ran wild, and the negroes became very much like them. At length, by mortgage, this property fell into the hands of Baron Mauá, the greatest capitalist and banker in Brazil. The baron had an adopted daughter, and she had a lover from the land of the Yankees; and the baron, like the sensible man he is, favored the love of the young people, had them married, and then turned over this plantation of four thousand acres to Mr. Hayes, for him to "improve."

It looked "seedy" enough, although that would seem an improper term for unplanted land — five years ago. But now the desert is beginning to blossom, and in five years more the empire will not contain a more flourishing or better conducted estate.

We were cordially welcomed at the station by our countryman, and, mounting a chariot which he had exhumed and renovated, — a curiosity, indeed, of Portuguese antiquity, — we were driven off to the fazenda.

A "fazenda" is, properly, a plantation; but the name is applied also to the house upon it. These houses are all in very much the same style. From a distance a fazenda, with its outbuildings, has the air of a fortress, being arranged quadrilaterally, with a large area within. This area serves as a playground for young darkies, a promenade for sheep, goats, calves, and pigs, a drying-ground for clothes, a receptacle for firewood, charcoal, vegetables, old tools, bottles, broken wagons, empty barrels, wash-tubs, and a vast quantity of filth, which might be of considerable service if incorporated into the land outside. In this instance foreign habits had very much improved upon native untidiness.

The front face of this fazenda was at least one hundred and fifty feet in length, being mostly of one story, with another added, sufficient for a few sleeping-rooms, over the middle of the long range. At one end was the kitchen, at the other the chapel. Between them ran a long, wide gallery, hung with family portraits. This served for hall, *salon*, and general purposes of family gathering, the dining-room and sleeping-rooms opening from it, and looking out upon the area.

There could not be contrived a more comfortable house for a hot climate. But there was an absence of piazzas and shade trees. Strangely, these are always wanting to Brazilian houses. There is no way of accounting for this singular omission other than by attributing it to the influence of negro blood, more or less of which runs in the veins of so many of the people. A negro, and only a negro, luxuriates in the sunshine of the tropics. All other natives of hot regions — the Bengalese and Malays, for examples — take every precaution against the sun's rays. When a white fireman on board of a steamer comes up from his watch, he always leans over the rail in the shade, where he can get the air. But the negro fireman comes up at noonday, under a vertical sun, and throws himself down to sleep upon a deck which would blister the skin of a rhinoceros.

This want of shade gives all Brazilian houses a forlorn and forbidding exterior. It must be occasioned by an Ethiopian love of sunshine.

A different taste is very noticeable among the people

of Montevideo and Buenos Ayres. In a climate of so much higher latitude, the luxury of shade does not seem so indispensable as it should be in Brazil. Nevertheless, their "quintas" are as tasteful as these fazendas are repulsive. There we find the most refreshing coolness in the very sight of the verandas, awnings, and shade trees, which are the invariable protectors against summer heat. Among those descendants of the old Spaniards there is no negro blood.

Arriving at the fazenda, we were kindly received by the charming hostess, whose agreeable manners made us immediately at home. Hospitality is a Brazilian virtue, and we were not surprised at meeting a numerous though accidental company around the table. It was not unpleasant to find that while the taste of her Brazilian guests had been duly consulted, the English education of our young hostess had qualified her likewise to please the palates of her husband and his friends. So we had a nicely prepared English dinner, while the Brazilians, neglecting our dishes, held to their carne seca, torcinho, feijãos, and bacalhao.

The first three of these articles are served together, carne seca being, what its name implies, dried meat, or, as we term it, "jerked beef," immense quantities of which are cured in Buenos Ayres, chiefly for the consumption of West India negroes and Brazilians. It has long been an article of commerce, giving employment to a large fleet of vessels. Torcinho is clear pork, or the fat of hogs, from which lard is made. Feijãos are black beans. These three articles, with various concomitants, in which garlic is never wanting, are stirred together and stewed, and thus form the omnipresent national dish. Bacalhao, or salt codfish, ranks next. Professor Agassiz told us that the people about the Amazon are so fond of it, that they will not use the delicate fish of their own waters, if they can get this greater delicacy from Newfoundland. Beef and mutton are generally tough and lean. When these meats are seen upon the table, they are so much cooked that the little juice they contained is dried up, and the meat is blackened like charcoal. In this state it is served as part of an olla podrida, with yams, cabbage, and garlic. The Brazilian cuisine by itself is an unmitigated abomination!

Early on the next morning we were all on horseback, prepared to take a survey of the plantation. We trotted leisurely through the cotton, cane, and mandioca fields, and then galloped over the pastures, and through the shady lanes, which intersect the forest not yet brought under cultivation, passing on our way the gangs of negroes going to their work.

No one will suppose that they were hurrying with any great alacrity to their forced labor; but there was no appearance of suffering among them, nor were the overseers cracking whips over their backs. They were generally singing cheerfully, and they invariably saluted Mr. Hayes, pleasantly as well as respectfully. "God be with you!" they said to us, and "God be with you!" we replied to them; neither black nor white man thinking of the full meaning of this frequent benediction, or how much the divine presence is needed by both alike!

When each reflects upon the condition of the other, we think that we can appreciate the sorrows of the slave; but we cannot counterbalance these with the bliss which springs from ignorance and from the exuberance of mere animal life.

On the other hand, while the slave must often look upon the white man with envy, — chiefly because he is better fed and clothed, and has less labor to perform than himself, — how very far he is from any possible sympathy with the woes which civilization entails! — disappointed ambition, unrequited affection, society's poisonous breath of slander, loss of property, the fruit of that very tree of knowledge which we are all so anxious to reach, and which, when attained, so often disagrees with our mental digestion, sometimes changing the faith of childhood to scepticism in maturer years; even the wisdom which grasps "star-eyed Science," receiving in return her "message of despair!" Is freedom from all this misery nothing to set off against the white man's superiority? And of these evils how little does the slave know in his own person! Therefore it is that he pities us as little as we envy him.

God be with us all, and give us all His greatest blessing — contentment! for most assuredly it cannot be otherwise than that happiness and misery are equitably distributed, according to our capacity for enjoyment or suffering.

It was a delightful morning, but the sun was already blazing far up in the eastern sky, so that we could not see all that we wished with comfort. But we were satisfied that our enterprising friend deserves and will attain success.

His system of labor is different from that of the good philanthropist of Rhodeo. His negroes are literally "worked," his theory being that, as labor is their condition, the greatest amount of work compatible with their health and fair endurance, is to be got from them. With this end in view, there is a judicious distribution of rewards and punishments. A sufficiency of rest and of time for meals is allowed, and Sundays and certain holidays are their own, but laziness is not encouraged in any shape. The result of this treatment, combined with an active superintendence, is, that this plantation "pays," while that of Dr. Gunning and that of Santa Cruz, which we afterwards visited, do not; and there is unmistakably a better and a happier look among the negroes of Mr. Hayes than among the others.

As we rode homeward, towards noon, we were sincerely glad that there had not yet been found time to cut down the forest trees; and it must be confessed that the breakfast-table was one of the very pleasantest of our morning views.

In the evening we were called out to see the negroes, of whom there were one hundred and thirty, of both sexes and all ages, at supper. We had dined sumptuously, and our dinner had been moistened by the flow of pleasant conversation, as well as by that of champagne. These negroes were feeding on carne seca and farinha, enormous quantities of which they washed down with cold water. As they sat upon their haunches on the bare ground, their huge mouthfuls were constantly interrupted by guffaws of laughter, the tops of their cocoa-nuts falling backwards, and their unswallowed food seeming to lie in a deep ebony dish with ivory borders.

And yet, poor devils, you are but little more than brutes, as you seem to us! But to-morrow is Sunday. You will put on a few clean white rags, and you will wear gay red and yellow turbans, and ribbons of all colors. You will drink caxache, if you can get it;

at any rate, you will dance and be jolly. We shall talk, read, and swing in our hammocks. We will all be happy — will we not? — in our way. On Monday you shall take up the shovel and the hoe, and trudge to the cane-fields. We shall go to town and be plagued by our business. We shall all go to our work, and have a hard time — shall we not? — in our way.

CHAPTER XI.

Cultivation of Mandioca. — Its Importance to Brazil. — Process of Manufacturing it. — An old Roman Catholic Chapel. — Negro Worship therein. — Muscular Piety. — Barbarous versus Fashionable Devotions. — Return to the City.

AFTER all that may be said of coffee, sugar, and cotton, mandioca is the most important production of Brazil, for by it the whole people live. In some of its various shapes it is always on the table of the rich and the poor. The root of this exceedingly prolific plant externally resembles the sweet potato, or the yam. Its vine is like a bush, and grows to the height of several feet.

When eaten raw, the mandioca root is poisonous; but when boiled, it is wholesome and palatable. Thus it is used in the everlasting olla podrida of carne seca, lard, and black beans. But its general use is in the shape of farinha, which is made after the juice is expressed.

On entering the shed where the negroes were at work, we saw the first process of grinding the root in an ordinary mill. All the juice obtained by this means was conducted into a vat. A great deal more was afterwards extracted by squeezing the pulp in a machine precisely like a cider-press. The remainder was then dried in an oven, and afterwards broken and sifted. The coarse flour thus obtained is called farinha. It is used without further cooking, serving the place of bread upon the table; and it is moreover made into a thick porridge, and thus eaten at all times. The juice is first converted into starch, and then, by a heating process, is hardened and granulated, and so becomes tapioca.

On Sunday morning the chapel bell called the negroes to worship. Certainly the church of Sapopemba was of the independent order. In old Portuguese times, the baronial lords of these domains were aristocrats in religion as well as in all else. Then the chapel had the usual fittings of images, pictures, and silver candlesticks, and a chaplain conducted services according to the ritual of the Roman Catholic church. But the riches of the proprietors took to themselves wings and flew away, and they themselves are mouldering under the slabs of the chapel floor, where they cannot see the desecration over their heads.

The pictures and ornaments are gone, but the saints in the niches still hold on, without arms and without legs; and a faded figure of the Virgin, now dressed in gay Ethiopian mode, still presides at the altar. For years there had been no religious services.

The present occupant of the fazenda, a descendant of those whose boast it was that they came to New England for the sake of religious freedom, cannot conscientiously do otherwise than allow this same inestimable privilege to his negroes. So they have organized a church of their own, and have chosen a priest from their own number. No bishop ever laid his hands on the pate of this venerable Uncle Ned; nor are his vestments of the approved priestly pattern. His change from a secular to a clerical costume was made by simply wearing his shirt outside of his trousers. This style, with the addition of a large black handkerchief around his neck, sufficiently distinguished him from the congregation.

The services were opened by a general shout, and then a long, silent prostration of all hands upon the floor. Then, at a signal from Uncle Ned, about a hundred blackbirds arose at once, as if from a cover, and commenced a chattering song, which must have been first sung in their native wilds. Sitting upon their haunches, which favorite position they have assumed as an innovation upon kneeling, they clapped their hands, wagged their heads, and rolled their eyeballs to this savage melody. The words were African, with the exception of the chorus of "Sancta Maria, ora pro nobis."

The clergyman managed his part easily, without the aid of books. After the conclusion of this act, he crossed himself in every direction, whirling about like a dervish, then threw himself down, and rose again with an elasticity evincing an acquaintance with "leap-frog" in his younger days.

Music again, and that always vocal, while the congregation, standing, beat time both with hands and feet, like David "praising God in the dance." Why not? It is His appointed way to receive homage from these poor ignorant creatures. When their uncouth ceremonies were ended, they rushed out upon the green, yelling and tumbling over one another, in a very indiscriminate way. But the turbaned wenches, who displayed extra finery, were "upon dignity," or they feared to injure their toilets. In some instances these were quite elaborate, and their wool was braided and kinked *à la Mozambique*. Some of the mulatto girls were still more barbarous, for they carried behind their heads those unnatural excrescences termed "waterfalls."

We thought of the liveried coachmen and footmen, and the splendid equipages, waiting at the door of an "upper-tendom" Church, — of the fashionable ladies sailing out with gilt prayer-books in hand, as they enter the carriages to go home, with such "simplicity and godly sincerity," talking of what they had seen, instead of what they had heard. Why not? It may be His appointed way, likewise, for them to worship, for they seem to know no better.

Dispersing on the green, the negroes went their way, some to their quarters, while others strolled into the road and went to visit their acquaintances on other plantations. They are accustomed to walk many miles to pay their visits on Sundays, notwithstanding their hard labor during the week. On the following day we returned to the city, delighted with our excursion, and grateful for the kindness and hospitality with which we had been entertained.

CHAPTER XII.

Wearisome Monotony. — Visit to an Imperial Domain. — History of the Estate. — Incidents of the Journey.— Hard Supper and harder Beds. — A Morning Ride. — Golden Fruit. — The Estate of Santa Cruz. — The Emperor's Wines. — Bad Economy. — Splendid View from the Dome. — Inspection of the Palace.

THE variety afforded by occasional visits to the country was a relief to the tediousness of a life which was becoming very monotonous.

The novelty of coast scenery had worn off, and the mountain landmarks, losing much of their sublimity, were regarded as little more than aids to navigation. The same classes of passengers were going and coming, a further acquaintance with their language not improving our estimate of their character; and, worse than all, the freighting business became so dull that it was often less unprofitable for the steamer to lie still than to be employed.

So it happened that I was quite ready to join two captains of the American squadron, with some other gentlemen, who had planned an excursion to the imperial fazenda of Santa Cruz.

Santa Cruz is now the private property of the emperor. It originally belonged to the Jesuits, who, at an early period in the history of the country, obtained a grant of this immense domain from the Portuguese government. On a rising ground in its centre they built the present edifice, which, with its various extensive apartments, served them for all their religious, educational, and secular purposes, of which last they made no little account.

When the grandfather of the present emperor established his court in Brazil, he found the Jesuits a strong antagonistic power, and accordingly he drove them out of the country, and confiscated their property.

Among other large possessions, this fazenda of Santa Cruz, with all its improvements, slaves, and cattle, fell into his hands. It was then, and for a long time afterwards, an immensely productive estate, the land being rich, adapted to pasturage and the raising of every variety of produce. It is agreeably diversified by rolling country, meadows, hills, and woodland, and nothing can be imagined as offering better inducements for profitable cultivation. The Jesuits had also a due regard to health, and must have taken this important consideration into account in selecting Santa Cruz as their place of residence.

Old King João availed himself of all these advantages, and not only enjoyed an enormous revenue from the confiscated lands, but so improved the internal arrangements of the building, that he made for himself a spacious and comfortable palace. Here, sensible old king that he was, he passed most of his time, until he went home again to Portugal.

His son, Pedro I., the first emperor of Brazil, likewise lived here very comfortably, and derived many milreas from the sweat of the negroes and the hides and tallow of the cattle.

When the present emperor ascended the throne, he, too, delighted in Santa Cruz. Here his first children were born; but here, also, his first-born little prince died; and from that day, very many years ago, neither the emperor nor the empress has entered the doors of the palace.

This, in a few words, is the history, as it was told us, of Santa Cruz.

The distance of the fazenda from Rio de Janeiro is about fifty miles. In former times, when it was a royal residence, it was connected with the city by a good carriage road, which at present is sadly out of repair, and for the last few miles has dwindled down to little better than a bridle path.

The first part of the journey is made by railroad. We left the cars at Sapopemba, whence the diligence conveyed us six miles to Campo Grande, a small village with a large name. According to the literal meaning of the words, it is in a "large field." The public buildings consist of one church, and the private property of one *venda*. The inhabitants are many — the landlord, his wife, two or three sons and daughters, and millions of fleas.

We ordered a supper of boiled eggs, for these are the only articles of food that a Brazilian cook cannot spoil. Grease and garlic cannot penetrate the shells. But even eggs are unreliable. These people have no idea of a difference in them, but they use them in all conditions of age, and sometimes in the transition stage of being. Coffee is always good, and generally at the *vendas* hard biscuit is to be had. Rice is abundant, but no persuasion will prevent the cooks from flavoring it with lard and garlic: unfortunately, it cannot be boiled in a shell.

We managed the supper pretty well; and though it was inclined to "lie hard upon our stomachs," it did not lie so hard as our backs lay upon the beds, which were surely spread with boiler iron sheets. We would not have cared so much if they had been level. It was of the ridges, which lay across them like crow-bars, that we complained.

At night the population came out *en masse*, delighted to welcome us with the gayest hop-skip-and-jump imaginable. It will be remembered that sailors seldom swear; but on this memorable night there were certainly some expressions of impatience.

Morning dawned upon us not a whit too soon. After the refreshment of a bath at the fountain, that partly compensated for the want of sleep, we were on horseback at daylight, prepared for a ride of twenty-eight miles. It is thought that sailors do not appear to advantage on horseback; but we suffered less than in those detestable beds, and, being more accustomed to deprivation of sleep than our companions, we were fresher for the work, and "blew" them all in the course of the day.

We galloped off the first twelve miles before breakfast, and arrived at another little village, called San Antonio. While our meal was preparing, we walked out into the orchard belonging to the *venda*. It was a perfect little forest of orange trees in full bearing, for it was then the height of the season. A more beautiful intermingling of gold and green I never saw. The dew of the morning, yet upon the fruit, gave it a refreshing coolness, such as no orange can have even a few hours after being gathered, much less after being carried across the sea. There are no better oranges in the world than those of Brazil; and it seemed to us dusty and thirsty travellers, that none in Brazil could equal those of San Antonio.

After breakfast we continued our route. Fortunately the road was well shaded, protecting us from the sun, even at noonday. The ground was generally level, and easily got over. Much of it was pasturage, with here and there a small fazenda. Most of the land had been cultivated in former years, but was now run out, the planters caring very little about keeping it up. The soil, being generally thin, is soon exhausted; and as there is plenty more to be had, they seldom take the trouble to restore it by manuring. Orange orchards abounded by the roadside. The fruit was to be had for the asking. Even that ceremony was dispensed with, the trees themselves doubly inviting us as we availed ourselves of their shade, paying us with their golden offerings to rest beneath them.

Long before arriving at Santa Cruz we sighted the dome of the palace, and by and bye we came to the long avenue along which the chariot of old King João was wont to roll. Now, it is so badly washed by the rains, that majesty, or any kind of humanity, would be seriously inconvenienced to get over it on wheels. But our animals, smelling the stables afar off, cleared the big boulders at a rapid pace, and at four o'clock they brought us to the door of the hotel. It is really a hotel, and a very nice one, too, that is kept by the superintendent of the fazenda.

Having first enjoyed the luxury of a bath, we were served with a capital dinner; and, as I do not suppose the emperor will ever read this, it can harm no one to say that the wine was excellent, for the palace cellars are well stocked, though his Majesty never comes hither, and would never drink wine if he did.

Pedro II. is a poor economist. He receives four hundred thousand dollars per annum from the state, besides his own private income, and yet he is always as poor as he is generous. A great deal too much does his "charity begin at home." With his revenue he keeps up several establishments — his chief residences are at San Christovão, the city palace, and at Petropolis. Each of them, as well as this fazenda of Santa Cruz, has its *attachés* in greater or less number, for whom he must provide. But it is certainly requiring too much to ask him to furnish such choice wines, especially if they are to be sold as well as used.

The fazenda is the nucleus of a small town. One of the chief buildings is that of our landlord. Others are occupied by his deputies, the superintendents of different departments. The smaller houses, in long *adobe* blocks, are inhabited by negroes, bond and free. The scene was quite lively in the evening. Music and dancing were going on in various quarters, the bright moonlight giving a very picturesque appearance to the groups of negroes.

Early on the next morning the palace was thrown open for inspection. Our first thought was to ascend the long ranges of staircases leading to the dome or belfry, whence we were sure to obtain a comprehensive view of the country. Every other consideration of it was surpassed by its beauty.

As we looked eastward, the sun was just rising, throwing his rays across the plains over which we had travelled yesterday. We were embayed in the mountains. The Serra, generally running north and south, about thirty miles from the coast, here bends, like an ox-bow, to the westward, and then returning to its line, continues its course. In the south-east was the ocean, glistening like a mirror in the morning light. The lands of the fazenda were embraced in the bight formed by the bend of the Serra. Far away in the distance, from west to north, and thence to north-east, extend the plains and meadows, until they come to the base of the mountains, which look down upon them, and water them copiously with their streams. On these the sun now threw his light, bringing them seemingly nearer, so that we could trace them leaping over the cliffs before they attained their quiet level in the fields. There on their banks were feeding the immense droves of cattle that run wild over most of the estate. Certain districts are allotted to plantations; but by far the greater part is in undisturbed possession of the grass, and of the animals feeding upon it.

The negroes were beginning to crawl out from their quarters, and were travelling off at a slow pace to their labor on various parts of the farm.

Descending from the dome, we wandered through the apartments of the palace. These were large and airy, without any pretensions to splendor, or even to what we call comfort in our colder climate. Some of the floors were covered with carpets, which, so little used as they are, will long defy the ravages of time, as they have done thus far. The furniture was all of foreign manufacture. Part of it doubtless belonged to the original proprietors of the fazenda, and all of it must have been brought from Europe many years ago. High-backed chairs with faded gilding, toilet and card tables with spindle shanks, long-posted bedsteads, great oval mirrors with tawdry decorations, and many more such evidences of antiquity, occupied the rooms. The banqueting hall was the unaltered refectory of the Jesuits, and their immense kitchen required no change.

One room is sacredly guarded from the intrusion of

strangers; only the door was opened, that we might see the bed whereon died the little prince. Perhaps his parents believe the story that he was poisoned, and this may account for their aversion to the place. Not an article of the furniture of the room has been disturbed since the sad event; not even has broom or dusting brush been there.

CHAPTER XIII.

The Imperial Philanthropist. — Giving the Black Man a fair Chance. — School of Negro Children. — Music by a Juvenile Band. — Compensations in Life. — Failure of the Santa Cruz Experiment. — A Sanitary Scheme. — The Emperor's Obstinacy. — Cultivation of Tea in Brazil. — Fruit Gardens.

THE emperor is trying a grand philanthropic experiment at Santa Cruz, on a system somewhat different from that of Rhodeo, vastly more extensive, but unsuccessful in about the same proportion. At Rhodeo there are thirty-five negroes — here there are two thousand four hundred. In his way the emperor proposes to "give the black man a fair chance." The slaves are allowed Saturdays, Sundays, and all the principal holidays for their own time. According to a calculation of the superintendent, they thus have rather more than half the year to themselves. Instead of being fed by their owner, they have a daily allowance in money, according to age, sufficient for their support. Particular attention is given to the education of the children.

Passing down the grand staircase, we entered the basement, which is used as a school-room. At that early hour it was not occupied by the pupils for study, but a band of thirty or forty of them, of ages varying from six to sixteen, saluted us with music which would have been creditable to many an orchestra. They played the national airs of Brazil, the United States, England, and France, and several pieces of their own composition. One little darkey, of eight years, made a very comical figure under the lee of an enormous bass drum, upon which he played with great dexterity, keeping time, as all did, with his eyeballs. Music is the negro's inherent gift. When we think of his sufferings and degradation, we may offset a little of our sympathy by remembering that he always has this divine emotion: —

> "Whose soft, celestial accents steal
> So soothing through the realms of woe,
> That suffering souls a respite feel
> From torture in the depths below."

Be this true or not, music is no slight alleviation to the woes of the present life. Happy the man who can always call upon this constant friend; happy the negro who can whistle and sing at his work, and dance to music when his work is done!

There are several teachers employed in the school,

some of them priests. They seemed very intelligent, and devoted to the work in which they are engaged. Their observation corresponded with that of the teachers we met at Hilton Head during the war. They say that the young black children receive impressions more readily than the whites; that they are better scholars, and develop more rapidly up to a certain age, when they suddenly stop, and not unfrequently relapse into their former barbarism.

The men and women are employed in various duties about the estate. Many of them have the care of the cattle, of which there are eight thousand head, besides horses, mules, and sheep. Others are employed in agriculture and gardening, and many are hired by the neighboring planters. But there is a prejudice against Santa Cruz negroes, and they are employed only when other labor cannot be obtained. Mr. Hayes, at Sapopemba, says that they have been very unprofitable to him, as they teach laziness to his own people.

Notwithstanding all their religious and educational privileges, they are a bad set. The plan of giving them an allowance for food does not seem to answer well. They keep the money, and then dig their mandioca and yams out of the emperor's land; they kill his cattle, and occasionally, when they are interfered with in this mode of getting an honest living, they kill an overseer. Many of them have taken to a gipsey life, "squatting" about on different parts of the domain, and, if disturbed, hiding themselves in the mountains.

The consequence is, that this exceedingly valuable property, instead of producing an immense income, is a burden and expense to its good-natured owner.

The slaughter-houses of Rio de Janeiro are in the outskirts of the town, so that when the wind is from their direction a pestiferous air is breathed by the people. The beef that is daily killed, to supply the four hundred thousand inhabitants of that great city, is nearly ready to die before the slaughter is commenced. The poor, tired animals, having arrived only the previous day from their journey of hundreds of miles, starvation and the flies have left but little life in them. The quality of the meat may be imagined.

It is said that corporations have no souls; but here is one that, with all its schemes of profit, which would doubtless be large, has more genuine philanthropy in its head than ever entered the kind heart of the emperor. It proposes to hire the Santa Cruz estate, paying for it from one to two hundred thousand dollars yearly, with the privilege of connecting it by a branch with the Dom Pedro II. Railroad. According to this plan, the slaughter-houses near the city would be discontinued; all the cattle from the country would be first driven hither, and pastured till they are fattened; then they would be slaughtered, and an express train would take the meat to the city in an hour. But the emperor will not consent. So much the worse for everybody. Were this scheme carried out, much sickness would be avoided; nearly half a million of people would get good meat daily, instead of skin and bones; immense droves of cattle would have an elysium of green grass before their death; capitalists would invest their money profitably for themselves and for the public; and the benefits would be great and general. By the emperor's refusal, all these advantages and a princely income are thrown away, and twenty-four hundred negroes are kept in laziness, for the sake of an experiment.

Several years ago, when the production of coffee exceeded the wants of the world, the Brazilian government turned its attention to the cultivation of tea, and incurred no little trouble and expense in introducing it among the planters. For a while it flourished, and great hopes were entertained that it would become an important article of export. But notwithstanding the high duties on Chinese tea, the cultivation of the domestic plant has fallen off, so that the home supply forms but a small part of the consumption. Coffee had again taken a start, for all the world suddenly began to require more of it than ever before. Accordingly the tea-plant withered and died. There is still, however, a large plantation of it at this fazenda, and it is perhaps as profitable as any other crop raised upon it. Especial care is taken in curing it, and it has a high reputation throughout the country. We were served with some of it for breakfast, and it really seemed equal to the "celestial flowery pekoe," which old Houqua poured out for us at his hong in Canton, years ago.

Oranges, lemons, grapes, and strawberries abounded in the gardens. We were told that these were for the imperial household. If so, the imperial household is large, and we were happy to be included in it for a time. So we cheerfully paid our landlord's bill, "asking no questions for conscience' sake," but acknowledging our indirect indebtedness to the emperor for the pleasant trip, and for the many good things to be had at Santa Cruz.

CHAPTER XIV.

Rival Beauties of Nature. — Bays of Naples and Rio de Janeiro. — Description of the Latter. — Sublimity of a Thunder Storm in the Bay. — Ascent of Mountains near Rio. — Adventure of two British Middies. — A Shrewd Dentist. — Sharp Practice. — Summer Resorts.— Route to Petropolis. — Pleasant Illusion. — A Sea of Fog.

THE bays of Naples and of Rio de Janeiro are the rival beauties of the world. For thousands of years there was none to dispute the supremacy of the first. It is still as lovely and as grand as ever, for "time writes no wrinkle on its azure brow." Cities, villas, and temples still sit smiling upon its shores, and the burning mountain at night throws its lurid glare upon its waters, changing the serene sunlight to the almost infernal grandeur of illumined shade. All these years it had reigned alone. The bay of Rio de Janeiro, like a school girl kept from view, was blooming and bright, ready to "come out," as she has done, to eclipse the reigning belle. Now that they are both known to the lovers of the romantic and the picturesque, the western rival is more and more appreciated and admired. It is vain to institute a comparison between them. They are alike neither in locality, shape, nor coloring; only in the general undefined characteristic of beauty.

To one coming from sea by night, and finding himself anchored in the harbor at morning, there has been a loss not to be estimated — that of the most sudden change from Nature's bold sublimity to her softest look of loveliness. Most voyagers arrive from the north; but those are most fortunate who first see the entrance of the bay when coming from the south, where the coast is more mountainous and abrupt. Steaming along under these towering cliffs, almost in the surf which beats against their base, there is no sign of habitation, or of even the smallest nook for shelter, — nothing, till, suddenly whirling around, the overhanging "Sugar Loaf" seems ready to topple upon us from its height of two thousand feet. Then appears, on the opposite side, the fort of Santa Cruz, the guardian of the port, between which and the "Sugar Loaf" is the narrow channel. Here, where two ships can scarcely enter side by side, is the entrance to a bay fifty miles in circumference, with the great city seated in the lap of its verdant garden; all else — its islands, shores, and mountain slopes — dressed in summer's never-fading color. It is only at the harbor's mouth that the mountains approach the shore. There, they stand as outposts. Within the bay, they recede for ten or twenty miles, keeping guard beyond the garden spread out at their base.

But, at times, what a change comes over this quiet scene! Vesuvius, with all its forces of fire, cannot hold us in such wonder and realization of sublimity. No description can portray a thunder storm in this bay — none but that in Byron's thrilling words, when he stood upon the banks of Lake Leman, and saw, and heard, the "live thunder." So it plays and echoes here. Not losing itself, as in the Alps, and becoming silent in the far distance, — it goes from mountain to mountain; not across, but around the whole circuit. Now it bursts with startling crash, echoing loud, then faint, and fainter still, till it has reached the distant "Organ peaks;" then, leaping from one summit to another, it comes back again along the chain on the other side of the bay, and at last dies away on the shores of the sea.

The black clouds seem to have climbed up the mountains from their slopes beyond, and now roll over upon the plains in bodies of water, coming in big drops, then in streams, and at last in cataracts.

Suddenly, more suddenly than the storm came, does it pass away. The sun bursts forth with renewed splendor, and almost instantly the glistening tears of Nature are dried, and she smiles again, as fresh and joyous as ever.

At a short distance from the city is the Tijuca Mountain, which, from its easy access, is one of the favorite resorts for summer. The railroad ends at the base of the hill, and thence the ascent is made on horseback. Bennett's hotel is reached in little more than an hour from the city. Beyond is a very celebrated cascade, which, unfortunately, at the time of our visit, was deficient in the most important requisite for a cascade; yet the little straggling streams were playing over the great, smooth rock, which was generally the floor for the dancing of a large and noisy company of waters.

The Corcovado (or Hunchback) is often ascended. From its crest can be taken in, at one view, a fine panorama of the bay. The excursion is made by the romantic on moonlight nights, in order to be ready to see the sun rise. Practical people, too, who wish to avoid the heat, often adopt this method. It requires but a few hours to "do" the Corcovado; so it was one of the things to be done "at any time," and consequently one of the things we never did.

The "Sugar Loaf" is so nearly perpendicular that its ascent is very rarely attempted. Some years ago, two midshipmen of a British frigate, wishing to honor Her Majesty's birthday, started on the evening before, and ascended the Sugar Loaf by moonlight, carrying a flag and staff with them. In the morning the English flag was seen flying at the staff on the very pinnacle, while the two scratched and bruised middies were reposing from their labors on the sick list. The admiral had heard of their exploit, and sent for them to come to his cabin. The boys were at first much elated by his compliments upon their patriotism and perseverance, but were somewhat chopfallen when they were ordered to display their perseverance again, out of respect for Brazil. They were obliged to re-ascend the "Sugar Loaf" at once, and bring down the flag. Since this exploit, no other similar attempt has been made to take possession of the country.

Across the bay, which in front of the city is three miles wide, are the suburbs of Praia Grande and St. Domingo. Many of the foreign residents have their dwellings in these towns, so closely and pleasantly connected with the city. An enterprising Yankee, Dr. R., who, as a dentist, made a fortune from the teeth of the people, is doing the same thing "in spite of their teeth," again, by the monopoly of the ferry. He originated a company, procured all needed privileges from the government, and ordered ferry-boats from home, which, fortunately, arrived safely, notwithstanding all their top-hamper and apparent unseaworthiness. They are now in successful operation, the sharp practitioner being the agent and pursuing the tactics of an accomplished stock-broker. He plays the shares up and down to suit his own purposes, beautifully bamboozling the innocent stockholders; and he gains more money in this way than in a regular course of business. The doctor is one of the celebrities of Rio. He is universally liked and disliked, and the pleasant smile with which he receives the money and the curses of the people at the same time, is a study in physiognomy.

Small steamers run often to the various suburbs and towns on the bay. There is one of great speed and conveniently arranged for passengers, which leaves every afternoon on the route for Petropolis — that most desirable of all the summer resorts. This town is situated on the top of the Serra, at a distance of forty miles from Rio de Janeiro. The climate is delightfully cool in the morning and evening of the hottest midsummer days, and is delicious in winter, when only occasionally fires are needed. It is, however, subject to heavy showers of rain, that come with little warning. Here is the summer palace of the emperor, and the foreign ministers, with their *attachés*, make it their permanent residence.

No change can be imagined more refreshing in the heat of summer than a sudden transition from the tropical languor of the city to the bracing atmosphere of these mountains. The time spent on board the steamboat is but an hour, while we are carried fourteen miles on the bay, passing many pretty islets and the large Island of Governador. This is the most extensive and the most fertile of them all. Very picturesque were the faluas, some of them laden with fruit, as they passed up and down along our route, some working sharply to windward, and others with their lateen sails wing-and-winged, flying like birds before the sea breeze.

Arriving at the end of the steamboat route, we take the cars upon a short railroad line of twenty miles, carrying us over a level, swampy country, abounding in mosquitoes, to the foot of the Serra. Again we have a transfer, and by far the pleasantest. The carriage road for the remaining distance, built by French engineers, is a wonderful triumph over natural obstacles. The Serra is here very steep, but the road is laid out in a zigzag style, like the working of a trench in the approach to a fortress. It is perfectly smooth, being macadamized throughout. The outside is protected by a wall five feet in height. To each carriage are harnessed six mules; these trot briskly up the continuous ascent of eight miles, changing but once — a performance of which no horses would be capable. It matters not on which side of the carriage you take your seat, as at every few rods there is a turn admitting a full view of the magnificent prospect below. This is equally captivating, whether ascending in the evening or returning in the morning.

Generally the weather is more clear in the afternoon. Then, at every turn, the bay and its surroundings come into full view, and frequently the shadow of the mountains, falling over part of the land between their base and the water, makes one of the prettiest pictures imaginable. It is a favorite walk from the town of Petropolis to the brink of the Serra, where this may be seen in perfection.

On the descent there is a charming illusion produced by the fog so frequently hanging over the bay, at the same time that the air on the heights of the Serra is perfectly clear. Then the bay seems to extend to the very base of the mountains, and to be directly under us. The lower peaks and spurs of hills become rocky islands in this sea of fog. The illusion is most perfect to a stranger who sees it for the first time. For him it is a reality that he cannot doubt, until he descends into the mist which he so surely thought to be the sea.

Having reached the "Alto," three thousand feet high, there is a slight descent to the village. Then there is the evening excitement, as a dozen coaches rattle furiously down the street, with a blowing of bugles and a cracking of whips. Groups of ladies are waiting upon the verandas of the hotels, to "see who has come," and those who have come are quite ready for the clothes-brush, the wash-stand, and their dinner.

CHAPTER XV.

Petropolis and its People. — The Palace and Gardens. — The Coffee Trade. — A Profitable Road. — Among the Rivers. — Paying a Visit. — A Pleasant Drive. — A Bit of Sentiment. — Change of Carriages. — Plague of Flies. — Unwelcome Companions. — Jubilant Negroes. — A Jolly Englishman. — Mark Tapley outdone.

IN the town of Petropolis there are not more than fifteen hundred or two thousand inhabitants. Most of these are Germans. Many more live on the outskirts of the village, cultivating their little farms and vineyards. It is delightful to stroll about among them, and to transport yourself, with the air of a very little imagination, to the vine-clad fields of Germany.

The palace and gardens are shown to the public with much civility and attention when the imperial family are absent. The building is more convenient and comfortable than large or showy. In some of the rooms the floors and ceilings are beautifully inlaid with the various colored woods for which Brazil is celebrated. The gardens were laid out by Frenchmen. In most of the public and private gardens of the country the French taste predominates. In all of them there is a distressing characteristic of patch-work regularity. They are often made up of circles, squares, and triangles, the favorite borders of these little nuisances being inverted glass bottles. France is sometimes called "the garden of the world," but it is quite as true that England alone can furnish gardeners.

Petropolis derives some benefit from the immense traffic in coffee, which passes through, on its way from the back country to Rio de Janeiro. This will soon leave it when the Dom Pedro II. Railroad is continued and opened. It is connected with Juiz de Fora, a frontier town of the province, by an excellent macadamized road of one hundred miles. This road belongs to the "União e Industria" Company. Stage-coaches run the distance daily in ten hours, and carry many passengers over the road, which, at present, forms the only communication with the mines of Minas Geraes.

But the chief profits of the company are derived from the tolls on wagons bringing produce and returning with merchandise. In the last year there were carried over the road twelve thousand tons of coffee and twelve thousand passengers. The company owns one hundred and fifty wagons and two thousand mules. Besides these, the fazenderos often use their own teams in the transportation of their produce. When the União e Industria road was undertaken, the government guaranteed seven per cent. interest per annum on the capital. The investment proved better than was anticipated, for the stockholders have realized fifteen per cent.; and now that the traffic will be so much injured by the extension of the railroad, the government liberally proposes to assume the road at cost.

The town, or rather the post-house, of Entre Rios, in the Parahiba valley, is one half the distance to Juiz de Fora. For these fifty miles there is a gradual descent, and then commences a rise till the same altitude is attained at Juiz de Fora as at Petropolis. Down the slope from Petropolis runs the Piabana, and down from Juiz de Fora runs the Parahibuna. Here at Entre Rios (among the rivers) they both tumble into the Parahiba, which flows through the extensive valley of the same name to the ocean. The whole length of the Parahiba, from its source to its mouth at Campos, is eight hundred miles. For the last part of its course it is not navigable. Navigation commences two hundred miles from the sea, and continues uninterrupted for two hundred miles inland. In connection with the railroad, a large business will be opened for steamers, which of course must be built inland, to suit the convenience of this very peculiar river. At this place the railroad will soon intersect the turnpike.

The town of Parahiba do Sul is eight miles distant from Entre Rios. In the city we had often met Mr. W., an English engineer engaged in constructing this section of the line. He had urged us, in a very cordial manner, to visit him at his delightful quarters in this charming little town of Parahiba do Sul. The present was a good opportunity to do so, and at the same time to enjoy a drive over the justly celebrated União e Industria road. Unfortunately for me, if not for himself, my friend Captain G. was too ill to accompany me.

I left the hotel at Petropolis on a summer morning, the air so fresh that overcoats were needed on the top of the coach. It was exhilarating to be rattled along at such a slashing pace over this splendid road. Winding along through gorges in the Serra, continually descending, yet scarcely seeming to do so, we followed the stream of the noisy Piabana. Skipping and dancing along, now looking poutingly up from the deep glens, and then laughing gayly in the bright sunlight, this little coquette kept in our company all the way, babbling her pretty nonsense and playing her music on the pebbles. Little Piabana! I had no one to talk with but you; so I fell in love with you, and often wished myself in your arms on that warm day!

For the first part of the distance all was a wild forest. Sometimes we were walled in by perpendicular cliffs, hundreds of feet high, the rocks scarcely visible, so covered were they with cactuses, shrubs, and flowers. After every ten miles we changed our mules. In each team there are generally one or two wild animals, harnessed with the others to be broken in. There is, therefore, a grand "splurge" in starting from a post-house, each of the six mules being led off by a groom. When they let go, at a word from the driver, there is a jolly kicking scene enacted for the first quarter or half mile, till at last they all get settled down to a comfortable gallop.

As we descended into tropical regions, we came among numerous coffee plantations, extending far on both sides of the road. The formation of the land is very peculiar. It is made up of little hills, so that there is scarcely a level spot of five acres anywhere. The northern or sunny sides of these hummocks are generally devoted to coffee, while the southern, being more shady, are better suited to Indian corn. It is so much more profitable to raise coffee, that, although corn grows well, there is not enough of it raised for consumption on the road. Mr. Morrit, the president of the company, had this year imported two cargoes from the Black Sea, and two more were on their way from the United States.

As the day drew on and we continued our descent, the sun became scorchingly hot. Nevertheless, the rapid gait of our mules kept us in a breeze, and we were uncomfortable only for a few moments while changing at the post-houses.

At noon we reached the station of Entre Rios, and I left the coach, in order to diverge to Parahiba do Sul, the delightful quarters of our friend W. I was not sure of finding him at home, as his occupation often called him away; but he had told us that Mrs. W. was always at home, and if by any chance she should be out, the servants would show us our suites of rooms.

There are three houses in the town of Entre Rios, one of which is the *venda*, and serves as the station-house. This is surrounded by open stables, wherein are quartered three or four hundred mules. The consequence of their close neighborhood is, that the flies swarm in countless millions. These nuisances, added to the intolerable noonday heat of one hundred degrees, made our sojourn of two hours as far from agreeable as it could be. The invariable meal of carne seca, fat pork, and beans was served; but who that was anticipating a dinner of French or English serving, with its champagne accompaniment, could dine from this horrible mixture, stirred in with flies?

At last the coach for Parahiba do Sul was ready. It was a two-horse affair, with a back seat protected from the sun by a hood. This seat was already in the possession of a Brazilian lady and gentleman. They had a large quantity of luggage, and were evidently returning from a journey. Some of the boxes were upon the front seat, where there was also a little live piece of black female baggage. A bandbox was removed, and I was accommodated with a seat by her side. I regretted having left my cologne on board the ship. The hood of the vehicle was unfortunately at such an angle that an umbrella could not be brought to bear effectually, and I believe that the attraction of the little black wench at my side made the sun hotter than ever. My fellow-passengers seemed to consider me one *de trop*, and I certainly thought them three too many. As we went broiling along, the dust fell thick upon us, especially upon the colored young lady and myself. She began to assume an appearance of pepper and salt, as the yellow sand adhered to her shiny skin. We sweated (*perspired* conveys no adequate idea), choked, and panted; and there were maledictions not a few vented in Portuguese and in English, till the eight miles were finally accomplished. Then we entered the dirtiest little town imaginable.

We drove up to the door of our Brazilian passengers. They were most boisterously welcomed by a troop of darkies. The pleasantest thing that I had seen for some hours was the affection of these poor negroes. It paid in part for my sufferings, for I love to see the milk of human kindness, be the source from which it is drawn white or black. Bright shone their eyes, and what a display was there of ivory!

They fairly seized their mistress — who was a portly lady of more than two hundred weight — in their arms, and "toted" her off into the house, hugging and kissing her, screaming and dancing as they went.

My companions having left the carriage, I had the back seat comfortably to myself for the remaining distance of about twenty rods.

The coachman knew the "Senhor Ingles," for he was the only Englishman there. So he drove at once to his "delightful quarters." His dwelling was simply a one-story adobe house, containing two rooms and a closet, the whole concern not exceeding in space that of a ship's cabin, and with somewhat less than a hundredth part of its convenience or comfort!

Had he "sold" his guest? No; he fully believed that he lived in a sort of paradise! His wife was ill in one little room; the other apartment was the dining-hall, parlor, library, and everything else. The closet was the "spare room," in which he lodged his guests

(I was glad that G. did not come), and the kitchen was the largest of all, for it had earth's remotest bounds for its walls, and its ceiling was the sky.

W. was a combination of Micawber and Mark Tapley, hopeful and jolly under all circumstances, and most jolly when any one else would be most miserable. His reception was enthusiastic in the highest degree.

I was glad to find a basin of water in my "suite of apartments," and was soon ready for dinner.

Now, W. was fully persuaded that he lived not only very comfortably, but in considerable luxury. He had a singular preference for canned provisions and salt herrings. There was no meat to be had in the market; but he thought that "fresh meat was bad in this climate." He seemed to entertain a different opinion at the hotel in the city. It is true there was very little air in the dog-hole where he lived; but the "air always gave him the rheumatism." He was a very healthy-looking subject. He had no stable for his two mules; but the "rain did them good, as it also helped to wash the cook's dishes." Society? "Pooh!" said he, "if we had our own countrymen to talk with, how should we keep up our Portuguese? And as to church, I do love my religion; and when I return to England, how I shall enjoy it, from having been so long deprived of its comforts!"

To all appearance I fell into his vein for the time, and pretended to enjoy everything hugely, being privately as miserable as Mark Tapley himself could desire. Poor Mrs. W., to my great regret, crept from her bed, and did the honors of the dinner-table. Still, I thought that perhaps she was glad to see me. W. is off sometimes for weeks upon the railroad, leaving her alone, with only a black servant, and not a person who can speak her language in the place. "What singular creatures women are!" said W., as he smoked his pipe, after dinner. "Do you know, my wife is sometimes discontented here? For God's sake, what more can a woman want than she has, with every comfort about her!"

In the evening we walked out, and called upon some of *élite* of the town. One of them kept a billiard-room, containing a half-clothed billiard-table. Another, who was the merchant prince of the place, occupied one room for his dwelling and his office. We found him asleep on a pile of bean bags, in the midst of his other stock of coffee and carne seca, with the aroma of which the apartment was penetrated. The ladies we saw were chiefly Ethiopian.

On retiring to my "suite," W. cautioned me to close the window, awfully hot as it was. "They are a good, honest set of people here," said he, "but it is not well to place temptations in their way. In fact, I left my window open once or twice, and everything was stolen out of the house." As it was impossible to sleep with the window closed, I left it open, and sat by it all night, studying a treatise on engineering as attentively as the mosquitoes would permit. In the morning, not wishing to be subjected to such carriage inconveniences as on the previous day, I accepted the offer of a mule from my friend's "stables," and thanking him for his hospitality, — which he begged me "not to mention," — I trotted off to Entre Rios, and there awaited the arrival of the return coach for Petropolis.

THE DRIVE TO PARAHIBA.

CHAPTER XVI.

Immigration to Brazil from the Southern States. — Contradictory Accounts. — Benefit to the Country. — Evils of Amalgamation. — Swiss, German, and French Settlers. — A White Slave Trade. — Islanders returning Home. — A Pleasant Picture.

THESE sketches of excursions into the country have been given, not only with the intention of amusing, but with the hope that some practical hints may be taken from them.

Much has been said in Brazil of the prospect of colonization from the Southern States of the Union. Doubtless there will be an immigration to some extent, but it cannot be as large as many who are interested would have us believe. Up to this time (September, 1866), the number of immigrants has been so small as to be quite insignificant. There have arrived at Rio de Janeiro scarcely more than a dozen families, and there are probably not more than a hundred individuals in all. Some of these have already become disgusted, and have returned to their old homes. Others seem determined to persevere, and are confident of success.

On our route between Rio de Janeiro and Santos, the going and returning immigrants were occasionally among my passengers. The stories told by them were of a very opposite kind. Individual temperament, rather than a disposition to be untruthful, influenced many of these reports. According to some, who had been "prospecting," and were returning to procure furniture and agricultural tools for their new homes, here was "a land flowing with milk and honey." All that was needed was to clear out the Canaanites, and to have a colony of their own, with their own laws and customs, when they were to be independent of all the world.

The disappointed homeward-bound men told us that it was "a country not fit for a dog;" that the *bichos* destroyed the cattle, the ants ate the seed faster than it could be planted; there was either too much rain or not enough; the Brazilians were bad neighbors; no labor was to be had; there were no churches or schools; all, all was discouraging and cheerless!

We could hardly believe both; so we looked into their faces to find a solution for these discrepancies. Some of the men were young, rosy, blue-eyed, and cheerful; others were older, sallow, and morose. Accordingly we attributed these contradictions to the regular and irregular action of bile. Doubtless we judged correctly; for the centre of thought and motive is not the head or the heart — it is the liver!

A number of American immigrants have settled in Campinas, where they have already commenced the cultivation of cotton. More have gone farther south, upon the Iguape and Ribeira Rivers, having there, as a company, purchased a large tract of land, which they intend to plant with sugar-cane. Be these immigrants few or many, their presence will have some influence in developing the resources of the country. They will introduce machinery, and will bring their experience, which is a mighty power as opposed to the old, inherited customs of this slowest of slow nations. The Brazilians are already beginning to avail themselves of this by letting their fazendas on shares to those enterprising northerners; but they will not trouble themselves to be learners. All Brazilians are not deficient in energy. Far from it. Among them are shrewd bankers, astute lawyers, and far seeing politicians. But the fazendeiros who are rich have generally blundered into their wealth, or nature has showered the golden rain upon them, so that they could not very well keep out of its way.

But we speak of the Brazilians as a nation. Time only will decide upon the correctness of these opinions. It does not seem that this people can compete with the Anglo-Saxons, or with that pure Latin race from which they originated, and from which they have degenerated. If God did make "of one blood all the nations of the earth," it was a long time ago; and now, the blood is so certainly not the same, that He alone can restore it to its original purity. All the endeavors of miscegenationists have proved failures.

No people has attempted the experiment more recklessly than the Brazilians. Wherever their ancestors, the Portuguese, have gone, this has been their character. Thus, in India and in China, they have brought the human race down to a level scarcely a step above the orang-outang. In those regions the name of "Pariah Portuguese" signifies all that is low, vile, and beastly. Will Brazil rise from her present condition to be a fit member of the great family of nations, or will she sink lower and lower, until she reaches the depths of degradation? The world is now so shaken up that nothing can stand still upon it, any more than the earth itself can stop. If this people of Brazil cannot drag along their car of improvement, others will do it for them.

Years hence, it may appear that one of the results of our civil war will have been the repeopling of this land from the starting-point of the few dozens of Americans who have landed here. The first American colonists are now to take their turn in the experiment of civilizing this empire. More than twenty colonies have settled in it within the last thirty years — mostly Germans and Swiss. Few of them have been successful.

The Swiss are proverbially a homesick people. Many of these have returned — at least many of such as could afford to go home, have done so. Some few have accustomed themselves to their circumstances, and these have all settled in the mountainous regions, where they do not care to become rich. They are content with their old pursuits, such as they loved in their native land. Here, too, they can find rugged mountains and green valleys. True, there are no glaciers or avalanches of snow, but there are hail-storms and mud-slides, and goitres are almost as common here as in Switzerland. Happy Swiss, who can find so many things like home!

Nor are the Germans more enterprising than the Swiss. They have their little market gardens, and vineyards, and they can have sauerkraut and beer, as in *Vaterland*. As a people they do not care so much for the old home as the Swiss, but are more ready to make an old home of the new. Here they maintain their former customs in dress as well as in living. Hard, leather-faced-looking men they are, who wear their heavy frocks and blue woollen stockings, regardless of the thermometer; and straight, up-and-down women, with yellow, braided hair, — uncovered in rain or sunshine, — with short dresses and feet heavy enough to ballast them against the loads carried upon their heads. They all drink their lager beer, and gallop like troop horses at their Sunday night balls. They are happy in their way, without a thought of coffee, cotton, or sugar-cane.

France has her representatives, too; but they are scarcely better suited to grand purposes than the Swiss or Germans. Yet they perform their mission of introducing civilization of the French sort. They teach the people style in dress, music, dancing, economy, refinement, and last but not least, cookery. If they can make a revolution in this one particular alone, they will do their share in the work of regeneration. France has reached the highest mysteries of the *cuisine*, while Brazil is wallowing in its very pig-troughs.

But Frenchmen are not good colonists, in the sense in which we are just now considering the advantages from colonists required by this country. They are not enterprising; they do not care for plantations; they are seldom found asking for railroad or steamship contracts, or concerning themselves in any way with public affairs. They live together, love together, and quarrel together, in and about the Rua Ouvidor, in Rio de Janeiro, where there are the finest shops in the city,—a miniature *Rue de la Paix*. It has its restaurants, cafés, and billiard-rooms, and near it is the public garden. What more can a Frenchman want, unless it be his boulevards? These he cannot have, and so he sometimes sighs for them, and dreams, as all Frenchmen dream, of the day when his "little commerce" shall have made his fortune; pictures to himself the return voyage, and, as the Indian thinks of his far-off happy hunting-grounds, so the jolly little Frenchman makes himself happy in this present life in Brazil with the hope of a heavenly one—in Paris!

The French congregate mostly in the cities; but they wander about the country as pedlers, and are often met upon the road, trudging along under their packs of fancy goods, gayly singing to themselves, and talking to their dogs. What care they to think how bugs, priests, ants, custom-houses, and all other nuisances standing in the way of civilization and progress, are to be overcome!

The Italians cannot be considered as colonists. They come with their hand-organs, buy monkeys, grind away for a few years, and go home.

There is something very like a white slave trade going on with the Western Islands, but generally there is nothing objectionable in it. Now and then a Portuguese ship arrives with a company of these islanders. Notice is given in the papers that she is anchored off the Isle of Cobras. The intimation is sufficient. Immediately she is surrounded by boat-loads of eager purchasers. The cargo, mostly of young men and girls, is taken on board by the captain, with the understanding that on arrival they shall be temporarily sold for the price of their passages. It is just to these poor people to say that they are generally faithful to their engagements, seldom leaving the masters to whom they are bound until they have earned their freedom. They then commence work upon their own account, and labor with the greatest energy and perseverance to accumulate their little fortunes.

As might be expected, there is occasionally some immorality in these transactions. But many of the females come over with the express purpose of thus disposing of themselves, having very correct ideas of the morality of the country that gives them so good a chance of success. Many of the more respectable class marry and settle here, but the men generally expect to return. When there are enough of them who are satisfied with the results of their labor, they frequently charter a small brig to take them home. There is something very pleasant in the scenes of these departures.

The picture of the Plymouth pilgrims austerely

going to sacrifice themselves in a wintry desert to a religious idea, is familiar to us all, but it does not make us cheerful. I wish I could paint the scene of one of these little brigs getting under way, upon a canvas large enough to give expression to each happy face, and to the tearful, half-envious looks that peer up from the boats alongside; and then the waving of handkerchiefs, that last adieu, as the top-sails feel the breeze! It would be a good picture; for it would always be seen in the sunlight of a smile.

CHAPTER XVII.

History and Government of Brazil. — Unquiet Condition of the Spanish-American States. — Government of the Country by the Portuguese. — Emigration of the Royal Family to Brazil. — Their Return to Portugal. — Independence Declared. — Abdication of the First Emperor. — Accession of the Present Ruler. — Powers of the Emperor and the Parliament.

IN the early part of the present century, the history and government of Brazil would have been matters of greater interest than is felt for them now. At that time public attention was drawn to the South American colonies, which were imitating our example in throwing off the yoke of the mother country and acquiring national independence. This they gained, and we have seen how little some of them deserved a liberty which they so speedily desecrated and converted into anarchy.

Revolutions, "pronouncings," and "declarations" have succeeded each other so rapidly, that we are tired of hearing of them; and the politics of the whole southern continent are regarded by us with less interest than the triumph or defeat of a temperance law in one of our own states. Indeed, it is quite useless for people to waste their time in reading about these oft-repeated convulsions; for a single year may give a different aspect to the whole, and it would require a good memory to treasure up the story of all their counter-revolutions. Such a faculty might be more usefully employed.

Still, the history of these states affords a lesson to such enthusiasts as think to revolutionize the world in a day; to those who expect to reap the fruits of liberty without planting the seeds and watching their growth.

But the empire of Brazil differs from the others, inasmuch as its emancipation from colonial dependence was more gradual; and the result thus far has consequently been more satisfactory. In common with all her neighbors, although not like those of Spanish origin claiming the name of a republic, her constitution is modelled after that of the United States.

It is nearly four centuries since Brazil was discovered, and though now entirely independent of Portugal, it has always been governed by the same royal family. For a period of its early history, the occupation of some of its seaport towns was disputed by the French; but they were finally driven off, and the country was ever afterwards governed as a viceroyalty of Portugal, until, in 1807, the two countries singularly changed relations, Brazil becoming the seat of government.

Portugal temporized to no purpose with Napoleon, having yielded to his pretensions until warned of the futility of such measures by the example of the unsuccessful servility of Spain. Then the royal family of Braganza took a step which astonished all Europe. It was regarded as cowardly, but in their helpless condition it was certainly politic.

It was in order to save bloodshed, and with the hope that the invader would spare his subjects in consequence of his own unqualified submission, that Dom João, after counselling his afflicted people — who desired to detain him, and would have maintained his rights at all hazards — to obey Napoleon implicitly, embarked in haste with his family. He bade adieu to the thousands who had assembled to witness the sad spectacle, and left his native shores to seek a refuge in this distant colony.

Thus the loss to Portugal proved a gain to Brazil. She assumed the first rank, and, after the general peace of Europe, still maintained it, the sovereign preferring to remain here, and to govern the old country with a delegated power for some years.

In 1821, the old King João VI. had become disgusted with the new world; and his enemy, Napoleon, having no longer possession of Portugal, he returned to his home, leaving his son Pedro to govern Brazil as viceroy. But the Brazilians, having once assumed the first rank, were naturally unwilling to be superseded again by Portugal. Accordingly, in the following year they declared their independence, installing the viceroy as emperor, with the title of Pedro I. The Portuguese made a show of resistance, but the whole affair was accomplished without bloodshed, to the general satisfaction of all parties.

To sum up the subsequent history of the Brazilian throne, it is sufficient to say, that the first emperor, on account of his unwillingness to grant the people a liberal constitution, was obliged to abdicate in 1831. Like his father, he took refuge in the home of his ancestors. At that time the present emperor was a child. The empire was accordingly governed by a regency until the year 1840, when Dom Pedro II., although only fifteen years of age, assumed the supreme power.

Upon the abdication of Dom Pedro I. the constitution was altered to a more republican form. The power of the emperor was limited; for, although he holds a higher title, and receives a salary fifteen times larger than the President of the United States, yet his prerogative is less in many respects. The veto power amounts to but very little. If an enactment passes both houses, he has a right to withhold his sanction at first. It is then sent back to them, and if they pass it again, even by no greater majority than before, it becomes a law. The lower house is elected from the various provinces, very much as our House of Representatives is chosen, but the senators are elected for life, or during good behavior. They are dignified with titles which are not hereditary.

CHAPTER XVIII.

The Monroe Doctrine. — Forms of Government. — Foreign Enterprise in Brazil. — Improvement of the Capital. — Gratitude to a Benefactor. — Iron-clads and Torpedoes. — A "Confederate" Speculation. — A "Slow" People. — The three Professions — Adaptation of Religions. — Missionary Effort in Brazil.

JUST now with us there is a great political catch word called the "Monroe Doctrine." Some people imagine it to mean the annexation of the whole western continent to the United States. They might reflect, from the experience we have lately had, that a ship loaded too heavily at both ends is liable to "break her back." But let the Monroe Doctrine in its modified sense be extended to Brazil. Let us make an American state of it, without the process of annexation.

No matter what the form of government may be, for the theory of this is better than our own, while in practice it is perhaps worse. A limited monarchy of the mildest type, a Senate elected for life, subject to impeachment, and a House of Representatives chosen periodically by the people, form a system which is certainly free from some of the objections raised against ours.

But let the government, the custom-house, the post-office, and the courts be directed by North American intellects, the soil be cultivated by North American energy and machinery, down will go the tottering relics of barbarism; and as the Indians have died away from among us, and the Africans are now perishing, so will this composite, mongrel, effete race disappear from the world. It is destiny. Philanthropy, philosophy, and religions, are but egg-shells on the track of the irresistible engine — fate!

Even now there is scarcely undertaken an enterprise of the least importance that is not conceived and executed by foreigners. A few years ago there was not a drain in the city of Rio de Janeiro; all the filth and offal were then carried on the heads of negroes to the water side. The stench was abominable, and frequent accidents from collisions were seriously ridiculous. The streets were then rather obstructed than paved with rocks of various sizes and angles, and melancholy-looking oil lamps glimmered only occasionally at the corners. Now, the city is drained very thoroughly; many of the streets are russ-paved, and are well lighted with gas. All these and many more improvements have been accomplished by foreigners. The natives are becoming disgusted with the increasing order and cleanliness.

But there is one public work to the credit of which a Brazilian is fairly entitled — the aqueduct. This is a fine piece of architecture. The grateful countrymen of the man who conceived it have deified him. In the palace square is a monument with an inscription to this effect in Latin: "While Phœbus in his course through the skies was burning up all the land and the people, Vasconcellos conquered his fury by introducing water into the city. Return, O Phœbus! and make your obeisance to this excellent man!" This is rather strong language, but it seems not to affect the sun, for he still shines spitefully hot, and bakes the ground over the head of Vasconcellos.

All the arms used in the present unhappy war with Paraguay are imported, and, with trifling exceptions, the navy has been built abroad. The "so-called" ironclads are the veriest absurdities of naval architecture. It is just to other foreigners to say that the contractors who furnished them are Englishmen. They have provided coffins for the poor Brazilians, and, if report speaks true, have pocketed more than half their cost. But then it is only just to the English to say that they are not concerned in another speculation, the credit of which belongs solely to some of our late "Confederates."

The Paraguayans, wishing to blow up the Brazilian fleet, employed some of these gentlemen to place torpedoes in convenient localities for that purpose. The Brazilians, naturally desiring their removal, contracted with other experts to take them away. It was productive of more business and of easier profits for these two parties to unite their talents, and to play into each other's hands. So, in a very quiet manner, they made a joint stock of both companies. The sunkèn torpedoes were then very easily discovered and removed; of course it was necessary to replace them with others, and when these others were taken up, more were to be laid down. The joint concern therefore did a very profitable business, the security of the Paraguayans and the danger to the Brazilians remaining about the same, at a trifling additional cost to both nations.

If foreigners conferred no greater benefit upon the country than accrues from such sharp practices as these, it were better for Brazil to be left to herself. It is true that Americans and Englishmen, in the real good they accomplish, are actuated as much as these roguish adventurers by a desire of profit. Still, while they have made fortunes richly deserved, they have greatly benefited the Brazilians at the same time.

But these people are slow to take advantage of the improvements almost forced upon them. The Dom

Pedro II. Railroad has been in operation eight years for a considerable distance from the capital; and yet, if you go twenty miles into the country, you will see respectable old fogies jogging towards the city on muleback, at the rate of four or five miles an hour, and you will meet cart-loads of produce and merchandise passing inward and outward. Everything is slow. The "law's delay," with us a great nuisance, is rather a luxury here. They enjoy its slow processes, as a Turk enjoys his prolonged bath. The original "Jarndyce *vs.* Jarndyce" was an affair of a day, compared to a Brazilian lawsuit. I know nothing from experience of the native medical practice, but if it is like their other modes of doing business, it cannot be easy for the physician to determine upon his medicine before the patient dies or recovers.

As for divinity, the seven years' study required for this, as well as for law and medicine, at the University of San Paulo, is short enough for learning the names of all the saints, and paying that attention to them which their worship requires.

In no country could the "three learned professions" be more advantageously dispensed with than in this. The law would seem to be only for vindictive people, who wish to pursue those whom they hate even to the third and fourth generations. The medical profession is much divided between allopathy and homœopathy.

The newspapers are full of their discussions, for which they must have a great deal of spare time; meanwhile, the people allow foreign enterprise to carry the palm away from all these disputants.

More successful than all their windy arguments on one side of the daily *Jornal do Comercio*, are the announcements upon the other side, of the wonderful "pilulas do Dr. Ayer," and those of Dr. Holloway, — the Yankee quack, by the bye, being considerably ahead, — and of the various "Sarsaparilla" compounds.

Be it remembered that this is a land of sarsaparilla; and yet these innocents are so gulled, that, instead of using their own pure medicine, freely offered by Nature, they will pay almost any price for imported molasses, water, and potash.

If the systems of law and medicine are adapted to the habits of the people, doubtless so is that of religion. It may possibly be heretical to entertain the idea, but it really seems to me that systems of religion, like styles of dress, articles of food and drink, tenements, personal habits, languages, and the local conditions of life, are adapted by the Creator to given periods and times, to various climates and races, and that they will continue so to exist to the end of the world, as they began somewhere very near its commencement.

Missionaries believing in the speedy approach of the

millennium, and considering themselves commissioned to hasten it, have been at work in this "field." The Rev. Mr. Fletcher was one of these pioneer Protestants. He travelled about the country occasionally, collecting materials for his book, and, as he tells us, was in the habit of paying for his food and lodgings with "the bread of life," by reading to the fazenderos and the slaves from his pocket Testament. His success was small, for it is to be feared that the people have believed as little in his Testament as in his book.

There are two or three missionaries still occupied in the hopeless task of converting the Brazilians. The Rev. Mr. Simonton, who is stationed at Rio de Janeiro, is a most enthusiastic and laborious man. He has acquired such a thorough knowledge of the language that he uses it fluently in his prayers and sermons, and publishes a weekly religious paper in Portuguese. The Rev. Mr. Blackford, at San Paulo, is another indefatigable missionary.

It is very possible, and even probable, that Protestantism may, by and bye, be the prevailing religion of Brazil; but it seems impossible that it should be the religion of this present Brazilian people. The whole tree must be transplanted. It cannot be grafted into this stock. The nearest approach to conversion of which the Brazilians are susceptible is reformation in their own religion.

CHAPTER XIX.

Influence of the Catholic Religion. — Its Power in Brazil. — Character of its Ceremonies. — Morals of Clergy and People. — Illustrative Anecdote. — Mixed Blood. — The Census. — Slaves Drifting Southward. — Extent of Coffee Cultivation. — Political Parties. — Anti-Slavery and Republicanism. — Succession to the Throne. — Character of the Emperor.

THE Roman Catholic religion is a mighty state engine wherever it prevails, except in the United States; and there it is often a scarcely less powerful engine of party. Governments encourage its superstitious observances in order to insure the fealty of the priesthood, and to make themselves stable by thus binding the people. With us, a standing army of tax collectors, postmasters, and editors, serves instead of priests, and they manifest an equally blatant loyalty.

The government of Brazil would not stand one day without the influence of the clergy. The ignorant masses would be the dupes of political adventurers, and instead of all this harmless mummery and nonsense, there would be bloodshed and hopeless anarchy. Still, it is to be regretted that the emperor's seat is not secure enough for him to put down, at least, some of the puerilities and absurdities. It is a humiliating idea that men should be made idiots in order to be good subjects.

We had seen the Roman Catholic religion in all parts of the world, and frequently observed how it was modified or intensified to suit national exigencies. We had seen it in Rome, where the headquarters of its ceremonies are admitted to be the headquarters of its abuses; but nowhere, excepting perhaps in Spain, is it so much like child's play as in Brazil. Elsewhere, sensible and educated men comply with some of its unimportant observances, from habit or from interested motives; but here, the most potent, grave, and reverend *senhors* "assist" with beautifully pious decorum at the wax-doll exhibitions and performances of miracles. On these occasions not a smile is seen, except on the face of a foreigner, or in the sly twinkle of a priest's eye.

The morals of the clergy are such as would be considered depraved in any other country than this. But morals, like other things, are comparative. Little hills would be mountains in Holland, and some of our mountains would be mole-hills if one stumbled over them among the Andes. It is true that the priests almost universally keep their mistresses, that they seduce many fair penitents, and are allowed all sorts of intimacies with married ladies, about which the husbands are not much concerned; for these people revel in such beastly impurities, that little priestly sins like these may be fairly looked upon as venial, and even as evincing rather a high standard of morality in the clerical profession!

If it is considered that these remarks upon religion and morality are overdrawn, the reader is referred to "Life in Brazil," by Ewbank, "*Le Brésil tel qu'il est*," and "*Les Femmes et les Mœurs de Brésil*," by Expilly. Ewbank devotes the greater part of his book to the churches and religious observances in Rio de Janeiro. He speaks, as I do, from observation; but his observation was more general and his opportunities more extended than mine; and his accounts are intensified in proportion. They are admitted to be true.

Expilly had seen some things in Paris. Nevertheless, this not over-sensitive Frenchman was shocked by what he saw in Brazil. Here is one of his stories of an enterprising Portuguese. In a condensed and expurgated translation I venture to repeat it.

The man was married, and was very poor — all his property consisting of a negro, a negress, and a milch cow. He undertook to make money systematically, by the increase of his "stock." Even with the aid of the cow in weaning, he could not expect more than one black harvest in a year. But mulattoes are as valuable as negroes. Think, then, by what double prostitution he succeeded in obtaining two in each season — one being the half of his own flesh and blood, the other belonging in the same proportion to his wife! So it went on, year after year, the children being sold when of suitable age; and by this commerce the worthy couple lived and prospered! It does not appear that the affair "excited remark" in the neighborhood.

Some years ago, when a census was to be taken, it was proposed to divide the classes of the community, and to enumerate separately the white, black, and mixed. The Brazilians themselves laughed at the imbecile who wasted his ink in the suggestion. "Mixed!" There is black blood everywhere stirred in; compounded over and over again, like an apothecary's preparation. African blood runs freely through marble halls, as well as in the lowest gutters, and Indian blood swells the general current. There is no distinction between white and black, or any of the intermediate colors, which can act as a bar to social intercourse or political advancement.

The whole population of Brazil, according to the last census, was 9,083,755, of whom 1,357,416 were slaves; of the remaining 7,726,339, called "free," it was wisely determined to make no further classification.

The warm and cold regions of the southern hemisphere being the opposites of ours, it would naturally be supposed that the majority of the slaves would be found in the north. It has been always conceded that if slave labor is profitable anywhere, it is so in the hottest districts of a country. Thus it was proved to be in the United States, where it was first abolished in the north, from motives of economy rather than of humanity. In Brazil it would at first appear that the rule of climate is not the same; but the existence of a greater number of slaves in the more temperate part of the empire is easily explained.

The northern provinces have partially freed themselves from slavery; not because it was not a paying institution to them, but because it paid so much better in the middle and southern parts of the country. Therefore the temptation to sell their slaves was irresistible to the northerners, who are now manifesting a great deal of virtuous indignation at the sins of the people who paid them so liberally for what, at the time, they were perfectly willing to consider as "property."

There is consequently a political anti-slavery party. It is constantly pressing its views on the government, and will doubtless be ultimately successful. It is made up from the provinces around the equator, extending from Amazonas to Pernambuco; while the more southern districts of Bahia and Rio de Janeiro, as well as the almost temperate regions from San Paulo to the borders of Paraguay, still hold on to the "institution" with South Carolinian pertinacity. In our contest both sides appealed to the Bible. Here the church furnishes arguments for either.

Brazil, however, has not such difficulties to overcome as those encountered in the United States. There is no appalling question of races to meet — no such problem here as we are now solving — whether distinct races shall live harmoniously, working, voting, and governing together, or whether the weaker race shall succumb before the superior. Here the general fusion, already so far advanced, will be complete, and we may predict the annihilation of the whole unnatural mixture, rather than that of either of its ingredients.

The diminution of slavery in the northern provinces, as has been observed, was owing to the demand for negroes farther south. This was occasioned by a sudden revolution of the taste of the world in favor of coffee, not long ago. Many of us can remember the time when the chief supplies of this article came from Java and Sumatra. A very little was derived from Mocha, and a larger quantity, though of an inferior quality, was grown in the West India Islands and on the Spanish Main.

At that time sugar was the chief staple of Brazil. It was made in all parts of the empire where the climate would allow the cultivation of the cane. Then came a time of great depression for coffee, so that the price for which it was sold was not sufficient to pay for the cost of raising it. The production was in advance of the consumption. The cultivation, accordingly, was very much diminished. So great was the reaction that coffee soon became scarce, and consequently dear. The world seemed to become aware of its loss, and then began to consider what was before a luxury, to be a prime necessity.

No other country possesses such advantages of climate and soil, and of nearness to American and European markets combined, for the cultivation and sale of coffee, as Brazil. All at once the middle and southern provinces were planted with coffee trees, to the almost entire abandonment of sugar-cane; so that now these districts are supplied from the north with the sugar they require for domestic use.

In the year 1860 the value of coffee raised in Brazil was $40,000,000. During our civil war there was a falling off in the production, owing partly to the fact that the south-western states of the Union, the great consumers of Rio coffee, were shut up. For a long time the people of the northern and eastern states consumed very little of it. Nothing but its cheapness has at length reconciled us to it in a degree. By and bye, when we become accustomed to it, we may perhaps prefer it to Java coffee, as they now do in the west.

The increased demand has so stimulated the production that it has become difficult to obtain labor. The domestic slave trade is consequently very brisk, and the negroes are withdrawn more and more from the northern provinces. The foreign traffic has been effectually abolished. Not a cargo has been landed on these shores for ten years, so severe and so rigidly enforced is the penalty. The importation of negroes was connived at before, but Northern influence will permit it no longer.

The anti-slavery party is already a disturbing political element, which will accomplish its work by fusing with one of the great parties. Then it will be no longer a servant or an accomplice, but will aspire to the rank of master and principal, as it has done in the United States.

Besides the anti-slavery party, there are now three others in Brazil, all very powerful and nearly balanced —the conservative, the radical, and the republican. The two former are imperialist. They both favor a continuation of the monarchy. One is what would be called in England "Tory." The term "Whig" to a certain extent would apply to the latter.

The "Republican" party is not so named for claptrap or *ad captandum*, but it is *bona fide* what the term signifies. It proposes to unseat the emperor; to do away with all titles and all insignia of royalty or nobility; to take — as all the rest of South America and Mexico have done — the great republic of the North for its exemplar. This party, again, is subdivided between immediate and ultimate republicans. The former are for upsetting the throne at once, and tumbling the emperor off. The latter are willing that he should remain for the rest of his life, and then they propose to overturn his seat before his daughter has time to climb upon it. If they play this game they must be very prompt in their operations. For should that young lady once get established there, her enemies will regret their temerity or their delay.

The only surviving children of the royal family are Isabella, wife of the Count d'Eu, a grandson of Louis Philippe, and Leopoldina, wife of the Duke de Saxe, one of that great German family whose peculiar avocation seems to be the renovation of effete royalty.

While we were in Rio de Janeiro, the youngest sister became the mother of a little prince. The event was joyfully announced by the ringing of bells and the firing of cannon. There was greater excitement than the occasion seemed to demand, for the baby is a very distant heir to the throne, even if the throne shall have an heir. Isabella is the legal successor. In case of her death without issue, the crown will be inherited by her sister. The little prince must therefore rely not only on the poverty of French stock, but upon the death of his aunt and his mother, who are both very young ladies, in the enjoyment of excellent health. By the time that old age carries them away, the prince himself may die, or, what is more likely, the monarchy may cease to exist.

The emperor has a merited reputation for scientific attainments and philosophy. He is an admirer and personal friend, as well he may be, of Agassiz, who has been with him daily at the palace, giving him an account of his researches on the banks of the Amazon.

We attended some of the professor's lectures, which were delivered before a large audience in the university hall. The royal family were always present, and partook, in the highest degree, of the general interest. Their eyes were never diverted from the lecturer or his black-board. The expression on the face of the Princess Isabella was intense. It is far from being pretty, for it is masculine; but, if physiognomy tells anything, it speaks of intelligence, energy, and such firmness as can be dispensed with in the conjugal relation, but is invaluable in affairs of state. It is Elizabethan.

Upon some points the emperor is obstinate; but his general policy is rather of the *laisser-faire* description. There are many things going on which he does not see because he turns his head the other way. When anything perplexes him, he rushes into his library or his laboratory, or among his bugs and fishes, and remains till the storm blows over and the discordant political atoms settle down, after the little whirlwind has subsided. If he had merely a few scamps to deal with, he doubtless has resolution enough to bring them to order; but where there are such universal rascality and corruption, he thinks it scarcely worth his while to combat a system which he cannot overcome.

CHAPTER XX.

The War with Paraguay. — Disappointment and Discouragement. — Religious Toleration. — Festival of St. George. — A Military Saint. — Rank and Pay. — His Saintship Tried and Punished. — The Emperor in Farce. — Brazilian Superstitions.

THE war in which Brazil is now engaged was undertaken with high hopes of immediate success. The activity of the emperor raised the enthusiasm of the people, and his personal presence gave courage to the army. For more than two years, with alternate successes and disasters, this war has dragged its slow length along, and at the present time appearances are very discouraging. The Brazilians regret that they undertook it, but they see no honorable way of withdrawing without acknowledging a defeat. Even were they to accomplish the object of increasing their territory, and could they succeed in trampling Paraguay utterly under foot, they would be poorly compensated for all their loss of blood and treasure. The money that has been expended as much for "shoddy" and private emolument as for the war, might have been better invested in the internal improvements so much needed. War is generally a bad speculation for nations. They always suffer, while individuals on both sides are the gainers. Brazil has made this discovery.

The emperor still goes about, examining the dock-yards, the ships, and the machine-shops, while there is an air of dejection upon his face painful to behold. He is a learned man; but it must be remembered that all his knowledge is derived from books and from foreigners, who are generally unwilling to give him any information that would be disagreeable, however useful it might be to him. He has had no opportunity for observation abroad. He has told Professor Agassiz that the great desire of his heart is to visit the United States, and that he hopes to do so when this war is over.

Although a strict Catholic himself, he tolerates all religions. Still, he declares that there must be one for the state; and what religion can be better adapted to Brazil than his own? Certainly no other. A good son of the church, he is submissive to the priesthood. In return for his obedience, they exercise their influence over the people, keeping them loyal to the government.

One of the great holidays is the festa of St. George, the patron saint of the empire in general. Each city has a sort of deputy patron, whose worship is duly celebrated on his particular day. St. Sebastian has especial charge of Rio de Janeiro, and has his great day, like the rest. But when the annual feast of St. George returns, every town and hamlet, from the Amazonas to the Rio Grande, has its greatest procession of the season. The saint has his headquarters at the capital.

I do not know if this St. George is the same that has taken England under his protection. Here he is Colonel St. George; for, although he died and was buried ages ago, and Brazil is now enjoying the advantage of his intercession, his earthly image holds the rank of colonel in the army, and draws a yearly pay of three thousand five hundred dollars! Of course the priests draw it for him; and they pretend that it is all invested in jewels and dress for the idol.

Until the present year this buckram saint has been mounted on horseback and paraded through the city, following the "body of God," for his day is likewise the day of Corpus Christi. To our great disappointment, this part of the ceremony was not observed. It would be charitable to account for the omission by attributing it to the advancement of light and knowledge; whereas it is to be explained by a greater absurdity than the performance itself.

Last year the attendant buckled Colonel St. George's sword so carelessly that it dropped and seriously wounded the toe of a priest. The aid-de-camp and the saint were both tried for the offence, and both were found guilty. The officer was sentenced to imprisonment for three years, and the punishment of the saint was confinement in his closet and prohibition from appearing on parade in the procession of Corpus Christi!

As the expenses of the war are heavy just now, it might have been better to stop the wooden colonel's pay; but this idea was far from occurring to the priesthood.

So the procession lost one of its chief attractions for us. It was something, however, to see the emperor in a new character — something, too, unpleasant and revolting.

It was a blazing day in May. Long before noon the procession began to form in the streets. This was composed of the military and of all the orders of ecclesiastical and lay brotherhoods. Every individual was bareheaded, and carried a lighted torch, the flame of which was scarcely distinguishable in the intense glare of the sun. The streets and balconies were crowded with broiling spectators.

Soon after noon the procession moved along through the Rua Direita, the Broadway of Rio de Janeiro. At its head we could see, rising and falling, a great silk awning, preceded by boys swinging censers of incense. Underneath it walked the archbishop, the canopy being held over his head by the emperor, the Count d'Eu, and the ministers of state, all bareheaded. This humiliating act was performed to show the obedience of the civil to the ecclesiastical power. We were looking on from the balcony of the hotel, Professor Agassiz standing among the spectators. As the emperor passed, he looked up with the most serio-comic expression that can be imagined. It seemed to say, "You see, my friend, what I have to do; but I am rather ashamed of myself." He must have been glad that St. George was out of sight, undergoing his punishment.

The Brazilians treat their saints with a great deal of consideration, so long as the saints are well disposed towards them, listening to their prayers, healing their diseases, and prospering their business affairs. Then the Brazilian is a grateful being. He adorns the shrine of his benefactor, dresses his image in costly robes, presents it with jewelry, and worships it with the most becoming devotion. But if the saint is ungrateful, the Brazilian knows how to be ungrateful, too. If he or any one of his family afflicted with disease does not speedily recover, or if his speculations have an unprofitable aspect, he will pray the good saint with all earnestness to turn the tide of evil; he will pray up to a certain point — the very point of despair. Then comes a revulsion. Prayers are now exchanged for curses, and genuflections for square-toed kicks. Thus, literally, is the saint punished for his obduracy.

St. Antonio is the most general saint of the country. He has more people called by his name than any other; consequently his image is more commonly to be seen in their houses and shops. These images fare well or ill according to the health and prosperity of their owners. As trouble in this world is supposed to be more than a balance for joy, the St. Antonios upon an average have rather a hard lot. A very common punishment meted out to the saint is to strip him of his dress and ornaments, and then to sink him in the well. If the sick person recovers, or the speculation takes a favorable turn, the saint is pulled up, has a new suit of clothes, and finer jewels than before, with plenty of apologies for his bad treatment; and penances are undergone therefor. If otherwise, — if the sick man dies, or the money is lost, — then the saint remains in the well, and is very liable to have his head smashed with a big stone.

The church in Brazil, holding firmly to all the original superstitions of Rome, has allowed much of the African element to mingle with religion, as the people have mixed it with their blood. It adapts itself to the ignorance and weak intellects of the blacks, and allows them to practise charms and rites of Fetish worship, which are quite as innocent in their way as are many of the genuine old ceremonies and dogmas. The negroes are permitted to worship black Virgins, as being more to their taste.

There is a favorite and very pretty white image in the Church of the Gloria. She has performed many astonishing miracles, and pilgrimages are made to her shrine from distant parts of the empire. She was a patroness of the mother of the present emperor. Many times did the empress visit her, to be healed of her diseases, and the Virgin was very considerate, paying attention to her most trifling ailments. At last a serious illness seized upon the empress, so that she was too ill to visit the temple. A council was held by the clergy, to determine upon the propriety of inviting the Virgin to leave the church and visit the palace. After much debate, it was decided, that, for the sake of royalty, the innovation might be permitted. Accordingly, with all delicate attention, as well as with all pomp and ceremony, the removal was accomplished, and the Virgin returned the many calls of the empress. But mark how fearfully she resented the insult thus offered to her dignity. The empress died!

Certainly, in one sense of the term, the Brazilians may be called a religious people. Yet it can hardly be supposed that the better educated classes believe in the efficacy of all this mummery. Most of these may be said to be infidels at heart, while they are superstitious in conscience. As children, they, like all children, are believers; and though in mature years they sometimes go to the opposite extreme, the impressions of childhood are seldom entirely effaced. Thus the Brazilian through life practises the forms of his early faith, entertaining the possibility of their efficacy, and seeking consolation from them in the hour of death. The selfishness of their religion is exemplified ridiculously in their prayers for deliverance when in trouble. In such cases, in order to be sure of help from some quarter, the Brazilian addresses himself to the sources both of good and of evil. In a storm at sea, or when passing over a dangerous bridge, he constantly cries, "Good God, good devil! Good devil, good God!" besides invoking the aid of any saints who may occur to his recollection. When all is safe again, he is very forgetful of his deliverers; and well he may be, as the debt to them all would be too large for him to pay.

Occasionally, however, his sore distress wrings from him a vow. True, when the danger has passed, he regrets his rashness; but his superstition makes him honest in its performance. A few years ago, the captain and crew of a brig promised the Virgin that, if she would keep their mainsail from being blown away, they would present it at her shrine on arrival at Rio de Janeiro. The Virgin having kindly complied, the sail was unbent from the yard and lugged by these devotees through the streets of the city to the door of the chapel. But the Virgin having no particular use for a brig's mainsail, an arrangement in the way of commutation was made between the captain and the priests. The sail was redeemed for a moderate sum of milreas, and was returned to the brig, where it was more useful than it would have been in a church. Many shrines are ornamented with curious memorials of gratitude for recovery from sickness, and for preservation from accidents, attributable to the special interposition of particular Virgins. There are very many funny and disproportioned pictures of beds and their occupants, of capsizing boats and of runaway horses, occasioning people to be spilled upon the water and upon the ground. Legs, arms, and skulls have been broken; but they have been mended by the Virgin — with the aid of a surgeon. Accordingly, fac-similes of these various parts of the body, done in plaster and in clay, are among the chapel ornaments. Under each is a highly descriptive picture, and there is frequently a detailed account of the perilous circumstances in which the individual was placed, and from which he was miraculously rescued. The perusal of these pious inscriptions was often a source of great entertainment.

CHAPTER XXI.

Religion as an Amusement. — Habits of Brazilian Ladies. — Female Education. — Women in Low Estimation. — A Comical Mistake. — The Steward's Blunder. — No Fish on Friday. — A Good-natured Bishop. — Light Penance. — Professors and Students. — Source of Brazilian Vice. — Theatricals in Rio de Janeiro.

THERE is still another view to be taken of religion in Brazil — its use as an amusement. Rio de Janeiro would be the dullest city on earth without it. The men in their mournful black clothes, which they so much affect, would grope about their business in the daytime and retire to their dens at night, and the women would merely walk from their beds to their windows and from their windows to their beds. But religion comes as a relief to such monotony. The many chimes of the bells give notice that some solemn farce is being enacted every day, and the frequent holidays and festas bring out the whole population into the squares and the churches. Processions are as popular and as common as with us on the eve of a presidential election. In them may often be seen little children dressed as angels; and very pretty, though somewhat dusky, are these tiny sprites, as they dance airily along.

It is only upon feast days that the ladies show themselves much abroad. Sometimes they are seen in the cool of the evening, enjoying the universal feminine luxury of shopping; but they are generally little inclined to leave their homes and their windows. It is a common practice to send to the shops for such articles as may be needed, that they may make their selection without the trouble of leaving their houses. Although laziness originated this custom, it has the merit of economy, induced by freedom from temptation. The Brazilian ladies spend most of their time in leaning upon their elbows, gazing listlessly into the streets, or exhibiting themselves coquettishly within the half-closed blinds, tantalizing those who pass. Mirrors are often ingeniously placed at the sides of the windows, so that the old and the ugly can see without being seen. The young and the pretty do not so much resort to this device.

More attention is now paid to female education than formerly; yet there is room for a great advance in this respect. At present, even the better classes are generally proficient only in music and in dancing. Perhaps their taste for music is in a great degree attributable to the African element, and the graceful voluptuousness of their postures in the dance may be owing to the same cause. The consequences of such general ignorance among them are either a charming simplicity of manner, or an extreme of vice such as may be incredible.

The Brazilian women are almost universally regarded as playthings, and as the means of sensual enjoyment. They advance the fortunes of their parents by being sold in the matrimonial market when they should be at school. Differences of thirty or forty years between husbands and wives are not uncommon. Fidelity is promised at the altar as a matter of form, but its observance is scarcely expected. The husband is allowed *carte blanche*, or, better to express it in an allowable pun, *carte noire*, in these matters. At the same time he is very jealous of his wife, as he richly deserves to have reason to be.

On our first acquaintance with the business of carrying passengers upon the coast, there were some ludicrous mistakes. I once incurred the violent anger of an old army officer, who, with his family, had been among our passengers, by inquiring after the health of his wife. Thus we learned that what is considered ordinary politeness in the United States is excessive rudeness in Brazil. At another time we left Santos with a large number of passengers on board. Among them was a gentleman of about sixty years of age, accompanied by two little girls — one of them thirteen years old, and the other two or three years younger. When the sea became somewhat rough, the gentleman retired to his cabin, under the influence of sea-sickness, leaving the children upon deck. Devoting myself to their amusement, I took them upon my knees and told them stories about home, with my thoughts wandering there, as I played with their silken tresses and enjoyed their pretty smiles. In the midst of this pleasant occupation the gentleman came upon deck. With an expression of face which I at first attributed to the fiend of sea-sickness, he gazed upon us for a moment, and then inquired, in a singularly harsh voice, "Captain, are you married?" "Yes, indeed, senhor," I replied, "and have a daughter two or three years older than your eldest little girl, here. She reminds me of her very much," I added, as I patted the lovely child upon the cheek. "That little girl, sir!" exclaimed my indignant passenger, with a severe emphasis on *little girl*, "that little girl is my wife!" I immediately provided a chair for the gentleman's wife and another for her sister. Soon afterwards the party went below, and the steward reported that there was a great noise in their cabin.

That steward, by the bye, was an excellent fellow; but his negligence on one occasion might have caused us serious trouble, had not the easy conscience of an ecclesiastic befriended us. We happened to sail on Friday, and the steward had forgotten the day of the week. It was particularly unfortunate, as it occurred in the season of Lent. Descending to dinner, it was found that his otherwise well-spread table lacked the great essential, fish, which, variously served, should have been the basis of everything. To add to my mortification, a bishop was on board, occupying the chair at my right. There was no remedy but an honest confession and a cry of *peccavi*, coupled with a malediction upon the unlucky steward, who, a Catholic himself, stood trembling under the enormity of his offence. The bishop assumed a serious air; but, after a moment's reflection, his face beamed joyously as he exclaimed, "Then I must give indulgence to myself and to all the passengers; but you will suffer for it by and bye. But stop!" he added. "You may as well suffer now. I will inflict penance upon you. Give us all champagne!" The penance was performed with alacrity, and this proved one of the jolliest dinners ever discussed on board the "Tejuca."

As our route was that of direct communication between the capital and the city of San Paulo, where the great literary institutions of the empire are located, the professors and students of the college were frequently going and returning with us. The latter were from the *élite* of Brazilian families, and were a jolly, rollicking set of fellows, yet gentlemanly in their manners, and evidently well taught, many of them being proficients in the classics and in mathematics. Most of the secular students knew little, and cared less, about religion; whereas the young men intended for the church were trained to their calling so entirely, that they were ignorant of all else beyond ecclesiastical observances and the monk Latin of the Breviary. On being reproached by one of his fellow-passengers for their general ignorance of what does not immediately concern religion, a priest told us a story which conveyed a fair retort. There is a town in the interior called Belem, or Bethlehem. The divinity student said that he had found one of the best mathematicians in San Paulo so ignorant of religion that he was obliged to inform him where our Savior was born. "Ah," said the youth who lived in a polygon, — "ah, yes, I supposed he was a Brazilian!"

The clerical students are frequently of questionable morality, and not unfrequently of unquestionable immorality. It may be said, in extenuation of their most common vice, that it is hard for any system of religion to hold men in restraint when it is opposed by human nature in a tropical climate. Chastity in New England is not so high a virtue as it would be in Brazil, if it existed here, which it certainly does not, to any considerable extent, in men or women, or children who can walk. A clergyman once came on board accompanied by his son, and the old gentleman seemed to be as highly respected as if he had denied the relationship.

It would be unjust to attribute such delinquencies to the Catholic religion, when we know that they are not uncommon among Protestants in our own land. The vices and supineness of the Brazilians do not emanate from their religion, which, with all its faults, is the best they can have. Without it, as I have endeavored to show, there would be anarchy. He must be a careless observer of society who does not see that its pest in Brazil is amalgamation — the mixing of two bloods which the Almighty never intended to course in one current.

Actors and actresses, all over the world, are often regarded as of doubtful reputation. Certainly in our country this imputation is most unjust. But in Brazil an actress who is not a prostitute would be shunned, as unfit for the boards of the theatres. It seems strange that the city of Rio de Janeiro, containing more than four hundred thousand inhabitants, cannot support one respectable theatre or opera-house. I use the word *respectable* in reference to size as well as to morality. There are the large theatre of Pedro II. and the Italian opera-house, both of which the government endeavored to encourage. But

PARANAGUA.

neither a correct dramatic taste nor a love for the perfection of music in acting existed. Both these houses are large, commodious, and well ventilated, but they are closed for want of patronage. The crowd throng to two stifling little dens called the Alcazar and the El Dorado, where a company of strumpets exhibit themselves nightly for the public entertainment.

Every people must have something to quarrel about, some parties to uphold, either religious, political, or — something else. The inhabitants of Rio de Janeiro do not trouble themselves about high and low church, abolition, temperance, or women's rights. It would be amusing to hear any one advocate these two last Boston notions in Brazil! But there are the great Aimée and Lovato parties. The young ladies who bear these names are rival actresses, both beautiful, both sweet singers and agile dancers, and each possessing a multitude of lovers. Every play-goer belongs to the party either of Aimée or of Lovato. As they both appear together on the boards of the Alcazar, the rival shouts of, "Bravo, Aimée!" "Bravo, Lovato!" frequently interrupt the performance with their noisy clamor. The favorites are fired at with volleys of bouquets, till the stage becomes a perfect flower garden. Then the young ladies, with a view to economy, collect the offerings, smile sweetly upon their admirers, and pass the flowers out from the side door, whence they are carried to the front and sold again. Whole columns of the morning papers are filled with praises in prose and in verse, as well as with abusive criticisms of these actresses. The representation of the previous night is the topic of conversation on the next day, and gives rise to many loud words and awful threats, which never amount to much, for the Brazilians always stop short of blows and duels.

Besides these little play-houses, where the pieces are always French, there is a small Portuguese theatre, which the emperor sometimes, though rarely, attends. Such is the staple of theatrical entertainment for this great city. Religion as truly takes its place in Brazil with gaudy shows and imposing ceremonies, as it serves the same purpose, in many large New England towns, with class meetings and evening lectures.

CHAPTER XXII.

Personal Observations. — Writers on Brazil. — Ewbank, Fletcher, Agassiz. — Inducements to settle there. — Southern Coasting Trade. — Unsuccessful Attempt to Re-open it. — Sale of Steamer Tejuca, and Return Home. — Southern Colonists in Brazil. — Drain of Men and Money by the War. — Dangers to flow therefrom. — A Word of Caution.

I HAVE endeavored, as much as possible, to compress these observations into a small compass, and at the same time to give the reader a general idea of the nature of the country, and of the pursuits and character of its people, in most respects so different from our own. It would be unjust to the Brazilians to pretend that an acquaintance with a comparatively small part of their vast empire can enable any one to form a correct opinion of the whole. No one, who has written upon the subject as yet, has travelled over its length and breadth. Ewbank was the best observer, and a most graphic delineator; but his researches scarcely extended beyond the city of Rio de Janeiro. Mr. Fletcher has certainly produced the largest book.

In a few months Professor Agassiz and his accomplished wife will gratify the public with an account of their extensive explorations. Their work will be welcomed by the scientific, and by all who can appreciate unsurpassed descriptive talents.

Those who have read Mr. Fletcher's book will not fail to notice that either his prejudices or my own incline us to take different views. It will be remembered, however, that my observations are confined to particular localities, and the inferences of general character are chiefly drawn from what was seen at the capital, and within a few hundred miles of it. My business was neither that of a tract distributor, such as Mr. Fletcher's, nor one of scientific research, like that of Professor Agassiz, nor of colonization, for which purpose Rev. Mr. Dunn has made his explorations. I had no occasion to flatter the emperor or his people; nor could my position or merits deserve any notice from them, such as was due to Professor Agassiz, of whom, in passing, I cannot forbear to relate an anecdote which he may forget to chronicle. When the emperor was about leaving for the Rio de la Plata, at a very critical period of the war, in order to encourage the army by his presence, the professor addressed him a note, conveying his best wishes for his success and speedy return, adding, in a postscript, "If you have time while there, don't forget to bring back some specimens of fish from that river." Dom Pedro complied, and the emperor's fish are probably in the Museum at Cambridge.

If any value is attached to this little work beyond affording an hour's amusement, it is that of conveying some idea of the commercial character of Southern Brazil, and of the inducements offered to Americans to enter upon its coasting trade or to settle in the country. I have not dealt in statistics, as such are uninteresting to most readers. In wading through Mr. Fletcher's book, these may be found here and there; but the best compendium is a little volume written by Mr. Scully, editor of the "Anglo-Brazilian Times," published in Rio de Janeiro. It contains the most accurate information upon those points.

An American company is now being formed for the Brazilian coasting trade. A mail contract is guaranteed to it, and large hopes of its success are entertained by those who are interested in it. There are some towns south of Santos which make large figures upon the map; such as Canonea, Iguape, and Paranagua. The new American line is to take the place of a former subsidized line of Brazilian boats, once running to these ports. That was discontinued for want of patronage, and the company made a complete failure.

Several months had elapsed, during which there had

been no steam communication with those towns, and the newspapers were continually publishing letters purporting to come from their people, urging government or private individuals to put steamers again upon the route. I accordingly advertised my steamer, and sent notices to all the ports on the coast, long in advance of sailing. We made three trips, being determined to open the trade again if possible. The attempt was abortive, for there was not freight enough in all these voyages to pay for the coal consumed on one of them. The towns are all wretched little villages, and offer no inducements or conveniences for commerce. We found the people entirely indifferent to commercial enterprise. They were glad to see a steamer, as they preferred her to a sailing vessel, because of greater speed and better accommodations; but they argued that they required no steamers for cargo. They owned a number of small brigs and schooners, which they were accustomed to despatch to Rio de Janeiro with rice, and to Buenos Ayres with *mate* (the native tea). On arrival there, the cargo is peddled out from on board. They consider the saving of storage and of trans-shipment as more than an equivalent for despatch. On their return the same little craft bring whatever cargo is offered, the time occupied being a matter of supreme indifference.

Despairing, therefore, of success under such circumstances, I sailed for Montevideo in September 1866, and sold the Tejuca there.

Returning to the United States, we learn that a greater number of emigrants from the South than we had supposed, have lately gone to Brazil. The Rev. Mr. Dunn, a secessionist ex-clergyman, is at the head of the chief American colony. This is on the Ribeira River, a stream which enters the ocean near Iguape. It is navigable for light draught steamers, and if the representations of the reverend gentleman, who came up with us on one of our return voyages, can be relied upon, there are offered great inducements for settlement in that vicinity. Cotton, rice, and corn flourish abundantly, and all that is wanted is protection of property by government and systematic labor. At present, jealousy of foreigners makes a residence there too exciting to be pleasant, and labor is scarce and uncertain. It is the avowed determination of the reverend head of this colony, that his people shall keep themselves separate from Northerners. If any such should show themselves upon the Ribeira, they may expect to be driven away, as the Quakers were once ousted from the sacred soil of New England.

I have already called attention to the progress which Brazil has made in the cultivation of cotton. The labor question, however, is as great a difficulty there as it is in the United States. It is true that slavery still exists in Brazil, giving the native planters a great advantage. But this is partly balanced by their lack of skill and energy. A few southern gentlemen, who have emigrated with money in their pockets, have bought negroes, and already have large plantations in successful operation. But the majority of the emigrants are too lazy to work, and too proud to beg for any thing but a passage home.

Soon the pressure of the abolition party in Brazil, aided by the influence of England and the United States, will terminate slavery altogether. The shock upon society will not be so great there as it has been here, and the absence of distinctions of color will aid in incorporating the blacks into the body politic. Abolition will not cause the ultimate extinction of the inferior race, but the whole agglomerated mass of mulatto humanity will live together or die together, as the future may determine.

Labor in Brazil is becoming still more difficult to be procured, as the country is depopulated by the hopeless Paraguayan war. This war never would have been undertaken, had the cost been counted; but it is now persevered in through the necessity of maintaining the national honor. It is already telling severely upon the vitality of the empire, and is fast exhausting its financial resources. It was popular in the outset, when the conquest of Paraguay was thought an easy matter. There were some early kindlings of genuine patriotism, and the courage of the Brazilian youth showed itself inferior to none. But gradually, as the magnitude of the undertaking became apparent, and the stubbornness of the foe was experienced, the fire and enthusiasm died out. Recruiting for each succeeding campaign became more difficult. The levies are now forced, and the living material of war is becoming more worthless, as well as more scarce. The fishermen and the poorer classes of the seaport towns hide themselves in the mountains to escape impressment. The motley crowd of yellow and black vagabonds sent to become food for the Paraguayans' powder, or for the malaria of their marshes, excites more contempt than fear.

It may be fairly estimated that less than one half the money expended is for legitimate purposes; the larger part of it going to enrich speculators and politicians. As we are now paying the interest upon a debt contracted in a somewhat similar manner, we may sympathize with the Brazilians, who are less able to afford such luxuries. Heretofore the expenses of the government have been met principally by the custom-house receipts, all other imposts having been very light. When an internal revenue tax shall be levied upon the mass of the people, there is serious reason to apprehend that its enforcement, added to other disturbing causes already at work, will bring the government and the constitution into danger. It may be well for those who fear a similar catastrophe at home to reflect upon this, in considering the advantages and disadvantages of emigration to Brazil.

NOTE.

The towns of Iguape, Canonea, and Paranagua, which have been mentioned in this chapter, were founded by the Jesuits, who established themselves in Brazil soon after its discovery. The chief evidences of their existence at the present day are the ruins of old churches and monasteries built by these zealous missionaries.

CHAPTER XXIII.

Abolition of Slavery in Brazil. — Free Labor and Free Trade for all the World. — The Slave Trade Twenty Years ago. — England's Disinterestedness. — The Necessity of obtaining Laborers from Africa.

REFERENCE has been made in the preceding chapter and elsewhere to the system of labor in Brazil. A further consideration of it is naturally suggested by the news just received. While the last pages were in press, we have learned that a project has been nearly matured for the abolition of slavery in thirty-three years from this time, and that all children born after the proclamation shall be free. The desired end will thus be reached in such a manner that the community will be better prepared for it than were the people of our southern states, and consequently such suffering as has fallen upon whites and blacks with us will be avoided. Undoubtedly this action of the Brazilian government has been incited by England and the United States. These countries have now only to bring the same influence to bear upon Spain, and then, be it advantageous or not to the colonies affected by it, all nations will be on an equality as regards labor, and the white man everywhere, as well as the black man, will have "a fair chance" in this respect. When the slavery of tariffs and the tyranny of protection are abolished, another weight will be lifted from the back of free labor. Then it will arise in all its dignity, and wherever, on the face of the earth, intellect can nerve the arm, there will its force and superiority be of right acknowledged.

As the period of manumission in Brazil is so far distant, the present cost of labor and production in that country will not be affected by it; so that what has been said upon these points needs no revision. Even if emancipation had been immediate, it will be seen that other causes would give Brazil an advantage over the United States in the cultivation of cotton. But as slavery is to endure for so many years longer, whatever economy there is in it is to be added to these. If, in years past, Brazil had been left to herself, she would doubtless have continued the importation of slaves in such numbers that, however much it might have cheapened the cost of her productions, it would unquestionably have resulted in the extermination of the whites.

It may be excusable, in this connection, to introduce a view of slavery taken twenty years ago, at a time when no hopes were entertained of its speedy death, either in a natural or in a violent manner. There have always been various plans of philanthropy afloat in the world. If this one was somewhat erratic, it was at least sincere. "The greatest good of the greatest number" is sound republican doctrine; and to those who regard all races as included in the enumeration, this plan ought not to seem very objectionable. Certain philosophers, however, who pretend to admit that theory, have taken a very different course of action from such a one as its natural inferences would suggest. They seem to have considered that the best way to civilize the negro and to promote his happiness on this continent was speedily to annihilate his race, even if this desirable result could only be obtained by sacrificing half a million of white men. This costly offering, we all know, was made for the preservation of the Union; but there are those ghouls among us who felicitate themselves that it was for the realization of their one idea.

On my first voyage to Brazil, in the year 1847, the following letter formed a part of my correspondence with the "Boston Journal." The slave trade was, at that time, carried on in such a barbarous and revolting manner that any suggestions for its amelioration, even to legalizing it, did not seem inappropriate. In those days many of us distrusted the sincerity of England;

and this feeling is not yet entirely eradicated from all minds. It was thought that the British government, having been compelled by the persistent efforts of Wilberforce and his associates to abolish slavery in its own possessions, was urging the same course upon other nations upon the principle of the fox that had lost his tail. The sudden change of sentiment, when lately her own interests were involved, which induced her to take the part of that section of our country where slavery existed, fully justifies the opinion of her time-serving duplicity which we then entertained.

It may be remarked that, when this letter was written, the author indulged the idea that the African was capable of self-government, and that he might perhaps become in all respects the equal of the white man. A further acquaintance with the race at home and in Brazil, in the West Indies and in various parts of their native Africa, has considerably modified this opinion.

"RIO DE JANEIRO, January, 1847.

"The chief misery of the slaves, after leaving Africa, consists in their treatment during the voyage. Once safely landed, who will suppose for a moment that they are as unhappy here as at home, where they are born slaves, and made the tools of their savage masters to fight their battles, and offered up by hundreds at a time to grace the ceremonies of a feast, or self-sacrificed on the altars of their own abominable Fetish rites?

"So long as the tide of emigration flows from Northern Europe to the United States (and thither it will continue to flow for many years to come), Europe will not attempt to colonize distant Brazil; but Africa will do it, and is already doing so, notwithstanding all England's hollow-hearted and hypocritical interference. The doctrine I am about to advocate may seem strange to many readers; but wait before you condemn it. For the sake of humanity, and of eventually civilizing Africa, rendering its people happy, and spreading Christian truth among them, take off every restriction upon the slave trade between Africa and Brazil, for the obstacles thrown in its way render the sufferings of the negroes tenfold greater than if the trade were free. The number annually imported now cannot be ascertained; but I know that while we were in Rio (thirty days), four thousand were landed in its immediate vicinity from five small vessels. We are not informed how many were landed on other parts of this extensive coast in the same time. It is scarcely possible to conceive that one of these vessels of two hundred tons could have brought one thousand and five negroes safely, having had on board, probably, on leaving the coast, about twelve hundred, twenty per cent. being the usual allowance given to death.

Who can imagine anything more horrible than their situation for thirty days, while crossing on the warmest latitudes of the earth, stowed with the nicest calculations of a stevedore in that vessel's hold, living and dying packed together!

"The slavers are now so closely watched on the African coast that an owner makes his calculations to lose one vessel out of three; and if necessity demands it, no hesitation is made in throwing overboard *cargo* to escape detection! The consequence is, that the only requisite quality in a vessel is her sailing, old ones being generally used in the trade, as subjecting to less loss when captured. England has the credit of doing a great deal to stop the trade, from the circumstance that her vessels so strictly watch the slavers. Well, so they do; and we see the consequences. But does she this from motives of humanity? Her people think so, and so do some of ours. Let us see. She has now a want of laborers in her colonies. She has abolished the slave trade. Where, then, shall she get her slaves, or (if you like a softer name) her apprentices? By robbing the Brazilian who has paid for them, and stealing his vessel, and sending these negroes, with their native land in sight, to be *apprenticed* in the West India Islands. I have been in St. Helena, an island but a few days' sail from the African coast, where five thousand negroes, taken from

Portuguese slavers (which were broken up or used for the British navy), were waiting for English vessels to come and take them away to English colonies — *apprentices!* This hypocritical system of slavery is less defensible than its open practice. These 'apprentices' are necessarily life-long slaves, for the time never happens to come when, to use a nautical expression, they have 'worked out their dead horse.' They go on from year to year increasing their indebtedness to those who are really, if not nominally, their owners, and only find freedom in death.

"It is to be hoped that England will yet see her own interest in doing away with this abominable traffic. She will then, with a somewhat better claim to speak, be enabled to lecture Americans upon their 'great national sin.' Even then, it will be well for her to remember that she introduced slavery amongst us against our wishes, and refused, when earnestly solicited by the colonists, to discontinue the traffic.

"I have said that Brazil is destined to be colonized by Africa, and I think that Brazilians of intelligence themselves are aware of it. Their country will yet be peopled and governed by blacks. Then we can introduce arts, science, and religion among them on this healthy continent, while death will always be, as it has ever been, the doom of the white man who attempts to settle in Africa. When this is accomplished, the inhabitants will have a commerce of their own with the opposite coast; and commerce carries civilization with it wherever it goes. First enlightened here, its influence will be felt across the South Atlantic; and that land, impenetrable by us, will have its darkness scattered by the sun of righteousness, and its deserts will blossom as the rose. And this will be more speedily accomplished if the Brazilian slave trade is freely allowed.

"By the laws of Brazil, every slave may purchase his freedom at a fairly appraised value, and the masters are obliged to accept the price. Many negroes hire their own time, being still fed and clothed by their owners, leaving, over and above what they pay them, one half to three quarters of a dollar per diem for themselves. Thus, in two or three years, they can, and frequently do, become free.

"Now, open the trade. It will be then thrown into the hands of others besides the few capitalists, who only can now afford to run the vessels; the trade being made legal, suitable regulations can be enforced, as with our emigrant ships, in regard to tonnage, water, and accommodations. Ship-owners will be satisfied with moderate profits, and the value of negroes will come down to so small a sum that the slaves can purchase their freedom sooner than England's *stolen apprentices* can work out theirs. The slave trade will be the same, from competition, as emigration now is from the Azores and Cape de Verds to Brazil, vessels frequently arriving from those islands with passengers, who are sold by the captains into slavery (or any other equivalent term you may substitute) to work until they have earned a sufficient amount to pay their passages. They are content, for they are soon free, and happier than they were at home; and what hardships have they there to complain of, compared with the African in *his* miserable home!

"Could suitable means be thus devised for the negro's emigration, and had they knowledge of how much better their condition would be here, would they not gladly flock to Brazil upon the same terms as these less wretched islanders?"

Now, I do not any longer believe in such a grand missionary programme as this, but I do believe that Brazil cannot be supplied with labor unless there shall be a species of coolie trade between that country and Africa, which in many respects will not differ from the plan proposed. It is with great diffidence, and with a consciousness of its little weight, that I record an opinion opposed to that of my learned and scientific friend, Professor Agassiz, who thinks that Brazil is a country adapted to white labor. I do not believe that this is true, to a considerable extent, in regard to any country within the tropics.

In the British East Indian possessions there can scarcely be found a descendant of the third generation of pure English blood; and in those regions a white man never exposes himself to the rays of the sun unless protected by an umbrella — an inconvenient encumbrance when occupied with the shovel and the hoe. Everywhere, in hot climates, Europeans become enervated and unfit for toil. Brazil will scarcely form an exception to other countries of the same latitudes.

In the more southern provinces, and on the higher levels, white colonization may succeed; at least, if there is nothing but climatic difficulties to oppose it. Notwithstanding that an unexpected number have emigrated from our southern states, it is not to be supposed that many more will follow their example, now that they will find labor so difficult to be obtained. There is an immense area of land on this northern continent sufficient to attract our attention, and that of all Europe, before it is time to pour an overplus into South America. Black labor from the nearest market is therefore a necessity for Brazil, even if the result of its importation should eventually be a black empire.

There is a race of negroes from Minas, a territory

on the west coast of Africa, differing from all other blacks. They are of immense frames, and capable of great endurance. The women are finely formed, and by the Brazilians are considered beautiful and charming. Both males and females display a remarkable degree of intelligence. They are very clannish, speaking a language among themselves, unintelligible to others, and practising the rites of their Mohammedan faith from one generation to another, unallured by the tempting ceremonies of the Catholic church. As slaves, they are valued at more than double the price of other negroes; and as freemen, they are useful citizens, for they will work of their own accord as no other blacks will do, with regard to the future. These "Minas" frequently purchase their freedom, and return to Africa, often coming back again to Brazil. They sometimes charter vessels for this purpose, after the manner already described of the Western Islanders, who, without having been slaves, have worked out the temporary servitude into which they are sold by the Portuguese captains.

Therefore, as the want of labor is more and more felt, it will not be surprising if emigration companies are organized for the purpose of bringing cargoes of these people from Africa to Brazil, as Irishmen and Germans are brought from Europe to America, in comfortable steamers, at a small expense. Although, if due precautions should not be taken, they might, like Chinese coolies, be sometimes bought, or "Shanghaied," still there would be a great improvement upon the old system of the slave trade. The Brazilian government offers no objection to the modified traffic in white men as carried on by the Portuguese ships, which are continually bringing emigrants from the Azores. It would certainly be impolitic to oppose it; for these islanders are the most available and useful white laborers to be obtained, and they are of real service to the country; but the supply from this source is necessarily limited. There must inevitably come a more pressing demand for immigration. The Paraguayan war has robbed the country of its best free labor, and thousands of slaves have been manumitted to become victims for the same sacrifice.

But peace will eventually come; and then Brazil will need all the supplies she can obtain for her recuperation; then, with the permission of England, whose influence is still supreme, she may be allowed to import apprentices, coolies, emigrants, — call them by what name you will, — laborers, at any rate, from Africa, or, more probably, from China.

CHAPTER XXIV.

Plan of Emancipation. — Kindly Relations between Masters and Slaves. — Intercession and Forgiveness. — Future Welfare of the Freedmen considered. — Du Chaillu's Estimate of the Negro Race. — Conclusion.

THE following extract from the "Diario" (official organ published in Rio de Janeiro) of April 9, 1867, furnishes some details of the plan of emancipation.

"There is no imprudence in revealing to the public all the facts we have learned on the subject. Our determination is to enlighten the people as to the events with which they ought to be familiar, and not to imitate the sad example furnished us by some who remain silent upon the most important issues of the day.

"In our opinion the project which is to form the groundwork of future parliamentary discussion is now elaborated. Already is a step made which honors the intentions of the government, and will cause the country to be the object of the attention and sympathy of the world. The plan to which we allude has thus far been canvassed to some extent in the Council of State, where it was indorsed by an almost unanimous decision.

"The following, as far as we have been able to ascertain, are the bases of the plan: —

"*First.* — Slavery shall cease totally in the year 1900, that is, in thirty-three years hence.

"*Second.* — The state shall indemnify those citizens who may still own slaves at that period.

"*Third.* — From the date of the promulgation of this decree, all children born to slaves shall be free.

"*Fourth.* — Those children who may be educated in the houses of their parents' masters shall serve them till they reach their twentieth year, and will then be restored to freedom.

"*Fifth.*— There will be established courts of emancipation in all the towns to enforce the law and see to its proper execution.

"*Sixth.* — A fixed amount will be set aside for the emancipation of the slaves of the nation, and the same terms will be agreed upon to effect the liberation of the slaves owned by religious orders as may be made to purchase the freedom of those held by the government.

"*Seventh.* — There will be appropriated a fund for the annual purchase of a certain number of slaves, so that but few may be in bondage when the hour of general emancipation is at hand.

"Such are the features of the plan, and after due consideration we can promise its originators the esteem of humanity and the gratitude of the country.

"The opinion of the Brazilian people on the subject of slavery is already known. All detest the institution in its principle. Such demonstrations as have come to our knowledge prove that all our citizens are in favor of the spirit of the plan developed in the foregoing summary. It is looked upon as a skilful and patriotic solution of the great problem that has long weighed upon the mind of the country.

"Accomplished by these means, emancipation will be effected in Brazil without creating either a disturbance or a financial crisis. And if, concurring with the plan set forth above, the government favors the idea of spontaneous emigration, and furnishes resources to allow of its development on a large scale, the country will enter into a new era, and settle its future destinies upon a firm and glorious basis.

"Instead of an immediate revolution, we favor a slow, gradual, and easy transformation of ideas, habits, and the mode of labor. It will have been, not a panic, but a peaceful revolution, the salutary reform, regularly perfected, of a whole nation."

This is certainly a fair and equitable compromise between the opponents and the advocates of slavery, and, what is of more importance to humanity, it makes political ends subservient to the real interests and welfare of the negro. Whatever opinion we may hold of the deficiencies and vices of the Brazilians, as being in many respects in excess of our own, it is the result of my observation, and I believe that of every one who has investigated the subject, that they are generally kind and indulgent masters, treating their slaves with much greater leniency than has been practised by any other people, among whom the "institution" has existed in modern times.

I can call to mind many touching incidents of the kind feelings of masters and servants towards each other. Intercession, even from a stranger, in behalf of a slave, however much his owner may have been provoked, is never in vain. On one of our trips from Paranagua to Santos, several runaway negroes were put on board, much against my will, by the police, with a guard who were to deliver them over to their owner. They had deserted from his service several months before, and he had been at great trouble and expense to get possession of them again. After wandering hundreds of miles, they had at length been captured, and, it may be supposed, were now on their way to meet with severe punishment. They evidently anticipated it, for they appeared so dejected that our interest and sympathy could not but be excited. Encouraged by this, they ventured to ask me to speak to their master in their behalf, when we should arrive. Upon a promise to do so, they rose from their despondency at once, for they were perfectly satisfied that they would be pardoned.

On hauling in to the wharf at Santos, the master, a rather ferocious-looking fazendero (planter), was found waiting for his slaves. As he stepped on board, I invited him below, and then asked him to forgive the runaways. The favor was immediately accorded. He gave me his word upon it, and I know that he kept his promise. The happy negroes kissed my hand as they followed him ashore, and we said to each other, "God be with you!" I think we all felt warm under our jackets, and I cannot tell whose satisfaction was the greatest — that of the master who had conquered his temper, that of the slaves who were grateful for forgiveness, or that of one who, at so little trouble to himself, was able to effect a reconciliation.

And now, in the process of freeing themselves from the reproach which modern civilization has laid upon slavery, the Brazilians have manifested the same spirit of kindness to the freedman of the future with which they have hitherto treated him in his condition of servitude. Slavery has been so general throughout the empire, that no section of it is ignorant of the character, disposition, and requirements of the negro. Consequently, there are no zealous bigots there who have never had the opportunity to inform themselves regarding these matters. There was a strong anti-slavery party, but there were few, if any, of its adherents who advocated immediate emancipation. There were no demagogues who could ride into power upon such an issue there, nor was there any disposition to use the freedman as a shuttlecock to be knocked about by political battledoors.

The temper of the programme, as given by the "Diario," is far different from this. There is evidently a sincere wish to make the liberated slave a useful citizen, if possible. The negro is everywhere among the Brazilians. They understand him thoroughly, and have no need to go to Africa to learn what Du Chaillu tells us, and what universal experience confirms as plain, simple truth, divested of all pseudo-philanthropy and political sentimentalism.

"Whatever may be our sympathy, — primitive man, or rather the least gifted tribes of mankind, must disappear before the higher intellect. This is not a theory, but a fact. There are many causes to account for the decrease of the negro. I think everything tends to show that the negro is of great antiquity, and has remained stationary. The working of iron, considering the very primitive way they work it, and how easily they find it, must have been known to them from the remotest time; and to them the age of stone and bronze must have been unknown. As to his future capabilities, I think extreme views have prevailed among us. Some hold the opinion that the negro will never rise higher than he is; others think that he is capable of reaching the highest state of civilization — in fact, that he will become a white man. For my own part, I do not agree with either of these opinions. I believe the negro may become a more useful member of mankind than he is at present; that he can be raised to a higher standard, but that if left to himself he will soon fall back into barbarism: we have no example to the contrary. Though a people may be taught the arts and sciences known by more gifted nations, unless they have the power of progression in themselves, they must inevitably relapse, in the course of time, into their former state. Of all the uncivilized races of men, the negro has been found the most tractable and the most docile, and he possesses excellent qualities that compensate a great deal for his bad ones. We ought, therefore, to be kind to him, and to try to elevate him. That he will, in the course of time, follow the lower races of men and disappear, I have but little doubt." — *Du Chaillu's Lecture*, as reported in the "New York Tribune."

The ability of Brazil to make good her promises of compensation to the slaveholders, and to discharge her other pecuniary obligations, depends very much upon the results of the struggle in which she is at present engaged. An expenditure of nearly a hundred millions of dollars per annum does not offer a pleasant prospect for the holders of her bonds. They, at least, will expect to receive their interest, before the holders of slaves shall be entitled to the proceeds of a second mortgage of the empire.

NOTES ON THE PARAGUAYAN WAR.

THE Appendix furnishes a concise summary of the progress of the Paraguayan War to the period at which we left the River Plate. The contest has since dragged its slow length along, with varied and various successes and disasters, until now it is generally considered to be closed. When, however, the repeated announcements of this most desirable end, that have been given with almost monthly regularity, are considered, there may yet remain a reasonable doubt of it. Reference has been made to the disastrous effects which the war had produced on Brazil already. These have since greatly increased, and if there is not an actual as well as a nominal termination of the strife, the result must be a speedy depopulation and bankruptcy of the empire.

It will be seen that, at the commencement of the war, the national debt was disproportionate to the resources of the country, which, moreover, could not afford to lose a single individual from its productive industry.

The principal revenues of Brazil are derived from the customs; indeed, it would be impossible to collect taxes from internal and stamp duties, as is done so readily in the United States. That nation is even now laboring under the burden of a paper currency, which all its great resources have not yet been able to redeem. It can scarcely be expected of Brazil, that she should come out from a struggle, which has been so disproportionately severe for her, with a greater ability to meet her debts, or to return to specie payments. As in the United States, so in Brazil, the system of labor has been revolutionised. In the one case, slavery has been abolished without reference to the benefit or the injury of the negro, as a party necessity. In the other, after volunteers and conscripts were exhausted, the negroes have been magnanimously freed in many instances, on condition of going to Paraguay to be killed. The two races who have been engaged so long in this unjust war, were unequally matched in numbers on the one hand, and in physique on the other. The hordes of mongrel Brazilians who swarmed upon the River Plate were met by a people, few but determined, and possessed of such heroic patriotism as is seldom recorded in the annals of the world. There is but little of negro blood in their veins, for they are descended from the pure Spanish race, which disdained the beastly admixture of the Portuguese with the blacks, while it added to itself the characteristics of patient courage, and, it must be admitted, of savage cruelty that belong to the Indians.

From the time when independence of the Spanish yoke was so easily accomplished, in 1811, Paraguay has been the most peaceable of all the countries upon the South American continent. It has been nominally a Republic, though always spoken of as a Despotism. But whatever the extent of liberty which its people enjoyed under Francia and Lopez I. and II., they did not disturb the liberties of others. The great aim of their rulers seems to have been isolation from the rest of the world. Unfashionable as this doctrine is at the present day, determined as we are that it shall be abandoned by China and Japan, it had made Paraguay prosperous and contented. Our opinion of the character of Lopez is at variance with that which has been so generally accorded to him. It is true, that we had not the means of judging from personal intercourse; but among all the Paraguayan prisoners we met at the River Plate, and of those we transported to Brazil, there was not a single one who did not speak of him with esteem, and even affection. It is impossible that a man who could thus succeed in winning the hearts of his people, so that every man and every woman among them was willing to die for the cause in which they were engaged, could be so brutal and unworthy, in all respects, as he is represented by his enemies. Such a tyrant could not have lived in the midst of thousands of people, who are supposed to have been his cringing slaves—such slaves who formed a nation of heroes!

A glance at the map will shew the position of Paraguay, Brazil, the Argentine Republic, and that of the Banda Oriental or Uruguay, which three last mentioned were united in the war against the first. It will be more difficult to explain, to the satisfaction of all, the cause of the contest; but it may be summed up, on the part of Brazil, in the late convenient and widely used term of a "political necessity." The south-western, and the richest province of that empire, is Matto Grosso. It is so difficult of access from Rio de Janeiro, that a person on horseback cannot conveniently perform the journey in a month, and the transportation of merchandise by land cannot be accomplished without a difficulty amounting almost to an impossibility. Consequently, the whole trade has been carried on over the waters of the River Plate, and its tributaries, the Parana and the Paraguay, which latter passes through the country of the same name.

Complying with the duties and exactions for transit imposed upon them, the Brazilians had heretofore managed to carry on their trade with no slight inconvenience. Latterly, as their power increased, their arrogance and acquisitiveness augmented in proportion, until it appeared a very natural idea that Paraguay should be added to their territory, or at least should so be disposed of that it should offer no obstacle to her commerce. In order to carry out this project, it was necessary that an alliance should be formed with the other Republics, so that Buenos Ayres and Uruguay should aid the ambitious designs of Brazil, rather than unite against her, as they had done in times past. Circumstances favoured Brazil in bringing about this result. In 1864 there happened to be a great deal of ill feeling between Buenos Ayres and Paraguay, which was insidiously encouraged, for her own purposes, by Brazil. In Monte Video, the capital of Uruguay, there had recently been an election, in which General Flores and his party were defeated. The proper combinations having been made, a Brazilian merchant steamer, the "Marquis of Olinda," with a governor of "Matto Grosso" on board, infringed the Paraguayan laws, and was accordingly seized. This, excepting some minor provocations on both sides, was the main *casus belli.* Buenos Ayres joined in, according to agreement, and a Brazilian fleet gave Monte Video the chance of being bombarded, or of receiving Flores for its president, and joining the alliance against Paraguay. Monte Video had no other resource but to submit, and that, perhaps, not very unwillingly. For in her case, as well as in that of Buenos Ayres, the war was likely to prove, as it did prove, a profitable speculation.

By the implied terms of the treaty, Brazil was to furnish all the ships and money, and the great proportion of the men, and as both these cities became *entrepôts* for all sorts of stores, and as they were called upon to furnish provisions at remunerative prices, immense wealth poured into them, and they could well afford to risk their blood, none of which was needlessly spilt. If Brazil had invested one-half the treasure she squandered to enrich these mercenary allies, in constructing a railroad to Matto Grosso from her capital, she would have saved for herself her money and the lives of a hundred thousand of her people, which, like the cash, she could not well afford to lose. She would, moreover, have saved her good name, and the danger in which she now is, in her impoverished state, of being preyed upon by her late friends.

In the meantime, Urquiza, the governor of Entre Rios, a part of the Argentine Confederation, had promised his adhesion to the tripartite treaty. But his admirable tactics enabled him to avoid fighting altogether, and to sell horses, cattle, and produce, to the belligerents, to such an extent that his country prospered exceedingly. The results of the war may thus be summed up: Brazil, wretchedly impoverished, but with the object gained of a free passage to Matto Grosso; Paraguay, with its population nearly exterminated, but the remainder unsubdued, and ready, at any moment, on the withdrawal of the enemy's forces, to reinstate their cherished leader; the Argentine and Uruguay Republics, richer and stronger than ever. They are not sufficiently grateful to Brazil for the money she has spent among them, to allow her to annex Paraguay. It may safely be predicted that the last condition of the Brazilian Empire will be worse than the first, and that ere long the four Republics will unite to keep her commerce out of their waters entirely; so that Matto Grosso, if it does not become a conquest of Paraguay, must be approached, as has been already indicated, by a railway, to connect it with the sea coast.

From all the evil of war ultimate good will be educed for the great dominating race of the world. The ways of Providence, though inscrutable in their justice, are evident in their designs. Before the Anglo-Saxon the Indian of North and South America daily retreats, and in New Holland and New Zealand the savage is disappearing. Africa remains the home of the negro, where he is supposed to roam "free in his native wilds," subject only to be captured and sacrificed to gratify the cruelty of his chiefs. Climate is an insuperable obstacle to prevent us from exterminating the natives of these benighted lands, where neither sword nor gospel can penetrate. There, at least, until some great revulsion of climate arrives, will they exist, as their ancestors existed thousands of years ago, unimproved and unimproving. All experience teaches that they cannot compete in the battle of life on equal terms with white men; and, therefore, it is a truth, however unpalatable, that if they must exist among us, it must be as dependents of some sort, if not as absolute slaves. In the United States, where they increased more than a thousand per cent. in that condition, from the settlement of the country to the commencement of the civil war, they have since lost one-fifth of their number; and the Chinese emigration, soon to supply with willing laborers the places of the blacks, who will not work, will ere long doom the remainder to destruction.

In Brazil, as has elsewhere been remarked, the hybrids, chiefly composing the population, are an unnatural *effete* people who cannot long maintain their ground before advancing civilization; and in the Southern Republics lately engaged in the war, the descendants of the Spaniards, although immeasurably superior to the Portuguese half-castes composing the population of their ally and enemy, are entirely dependent upon Englishmen and Americans for all that adds refinement to their lives, and for all that gives the semblance of progress to their nationalities. There is progress among them, but it is for the ultimate benefit of their successors. We have paved and lighted their streets, covered their rivers with steamers, and opened up their country with railways, one of which, under the indefatigable energy of Wheelwright, is now stretching itself farther and farther, until it will reach and surmount the Andes, bringing the rich Pampas, with their flocks, herds, and produce, to the reach of the industrious emigrants who are already populating them. All this the great Anglo-Saxon race is doing, not for the benefit of South America, but for the occupancy of their own children, who, when all these Canaanites shall have disappeared, will enter in and possess the land.

APPENDIX.

THE MILITARY PROBLEM ON THE LA PLATA.

THE great war of the allies in South America, having for its direct object the overthrow of Paraguay, still continues. Of the Uruguay contingent of two thousand, not a man remains. Five thousand out of the thirteen thousand kept in the field by the Argentine Republic have lately been absent, and at San Luis have just given the finishing blow to one of those internal *gaucho* revolutions which are periodically waged against the urban power of the republic. The Brazilians, numbering thirty-two thousand, are patiently awaiting the return of the Argentine troops, and the attack of a column of eight thousand men, under Osorio, who are slowly working their way across the almost impassable wilds from Rio Janeiro to the eastern Paraguay boundary. It is evident that the allies are gathering their forces for a final blow, and we believe if Paraguay stands firm under the assault she has nothing more to fear.

At the opening of the contest General Mitré declared it would be a "*paseo militar*," and that it would take but three months to reach Asuncion. The Brazilians were no less sanguine. The expression of these ideas indicated a great lack of military talent on the part of the allied generals; for they were to assail a country which occupies an almost impregnable position relative to the nations around it. East, west, and south are streams that will float a frigate, while the northern boundary is a vast and impenetrable jungle, frequently overflowed by the freshets of the Paraguay and Parana Rivers.

The bordering territory, both east and west, is a virgin wild, while the southern Paraguay margin, selected by the allies as the vulnerable point, is a swamp whose deadly malaria keeps their hospitals filled with men, who rarely rejoin their regiments.

The internal elements possessed by Paraguay for defence were scarcely inferior to the external ones which nature has conferred upon her. Up to 1810, the foreign and native element had been mingling, until the result was a compact and homogeneous people; and the war which the desperadoes from the Rio Grande province of Brazil had waged against them had given them a desperate schooling, and conferred a warlike nature upon the present generation. Francia ruled from 1813 to 1840, and was followed by a still ruder despot, Carlos Antonio Lopez, who for a score of years fastened firmly the despotism in which Francia had trained the people. At the death of Lopez, his son, the present ruler, came into power. He found ready at hand a compact nationality, which had never known any but the channels which a half century of despotism had carved out for it. Foreseeing the present struggle, he mobilized the nation, built workshops, founderies, powder-mills, railroads, fortifications, brought the skilled workmen and science of Europe to his aid, and made the vast military camp of Paraguay a warlike unit. The country itself is filled with almost sufficient natural productions to support life, where the people are so simple in their wants and habits. Thus the Paraguayan camp of seventy thousand square miles, containing five hundred thousand inhabitants, was a formidable adversary to attack, especially if we consider that there is but one vulnerable point in its geographical position — a point which, up to this time, the allies have failed to approach.

Against all this the allies could bring no proportionate strength. The overgrown jungle, called Brazil, making war on a water line of over two thousand miles in length, has been forced to strain its young nerves almost to the breaking. The Argentine Republic was already exhausted in her civil contests, and Uruguay had been so depopulated in her wars that her first effort to maintain a small force in the field was also her last. Both the Argentine Republic and Uruguay also had to wage war at an immense distance from their base — nearly twelve hundred miles.

The financial condition of the combatants scarcely varied from the condition of the other elements of the problem. Paraguay, at the outbreak of the war, had a general revenue of $3,750,000; yerba monopoly, $3,000,000; tithes and land rents, $1,950,000; making a total revenue of $8,700,000. The floating debt of paper currency was $2,000,000, and of external debts she had none. Her accumulated wealth was immense for so small a state, and immediately available for war purposes.

On the part of the Argentine Confederation, Buenos Ayres had to furnish nearly all the cash that came from the republic, however little in amount. Buenos Ayres had before the war a home and foreign debt of about $29,000,000, while her revenues, balanced by her expenditures, were about $7,000,000. At the outbreak of the contest, the currency of the Bank of Buenos Ayres, which had originally been issued at $17 paper to the gold ounce, had already depreciated to $425 per ounce.

Uruguay was even too poor to give a decent outfit to her contingents. The state was already loaded with mountains of debt, which had been piled one on the other during her civil wars. From her, therefore, the allies could expect only what they received — nothing.

Nearly the whole allied force, then, was to draw on the Brazilian purse; from her were to come the immense expenditures necessary to carry on war at such a distance, and under such adverse circumstances; but even before the war she was heavily loaded with a debt of about $125,000,000; and to this she has added, up to the beginning of the present campaign, some $200,000,000 more. To all this she will add at least $50,000,000 before she gets out of this Paraguay trap; and when peace comes she will find that $375,000,000 is a very rude strain upon her resources — so rude, indeed, that it is doubtful if her revenues can pay the interest upon the amount.

Paraguay then was, as she still is, the superior in point of finances. To maintain one soldier in the field, it costs her twenty per cent. of what it costs the allies, especially the Brazilians. It appears, then, that internally, financially, geographically, and in point of topographical barriers, Paraguay was and is a compact unit of force difficult to assail.

The first combats of Tuyuti and Curuzu, on Paraguayan soil, taught the allied army that it had rough work before it. Curupaity, a very inferior fortification, and a mere outwork, has long held them in check; this taken, they will find their labors just commenced; and at Humaita wild work awaits them. The vast swamp into which the allied troops have been foolishly thrown is margined by a series of formidable earthworks, and they are attacking Paraguay where she is the best defended by art and nature. The only vulnerable quarter which might have given hope of success was the north-west, which was and is undefended and open to attack from the Gran Chaco of the Argentine Republic. Moreover, one of the parties most interested in the removal of the Paraguayan stumbling-block is Bolivia. Had she been properly approached by the allies at the outset, a Bolivian contingent of ten thousand men would have settled the question long since. It is now too late; Bolivia is enriching herself in a very profitable trade of war supplies, which she is constantly pouring into Paraguay, and which assist in reducing all her neighbors to her level.

It looks as if the allies were waging a contest that long since became hopeless. The quicker they close the war by treaty, the better; for the unnatural alliance between the Argentine Republic and Brazil, were their efforts successful, would result in an immediate war between them for the spoils, which both consider necessary to their territorial aggrandizement and future progress.

www.ingramcontent.com/pod-product-compliance
Lightning Source LLC
LaVergne TN
LVHW050529100826
845148LV00002B/487

* 9 7 8 1 4 2 5 5 1 9 8 6 5 *